SIR OLIVER MOWAT

A Canadian Christian Statesman
Christianity's Evidences & Its Influence

A CELEBRATION OF FAITH SERIES

STEVEN R. MARTINS
SIR OLIVER MOWAT

To my father and mother, who went to great lengths so that I could be a Canadian.

~ Steven R. Martins ~

www.cantaroinstitute.org

Published by Cántaro Publications, a publishing imprint of the Cántaro Institute, Jordan Station, ON.

© 2020 by Cántaro Institute. All rights reserved. Except for brief quotations in critical publications or reviews, no part of this book may be reproduced in any manner without prior written consent from the publishers.

Unless otherwise indicated, Scripture quotations are from the ESV® Bible (The Holy Bible, English Standard Version®). Copyright © 2001 by Crossway, a publishing ministry of Good News Publishers. Used by permission. All rights reserved.

Editor: Keziah Van Vliet
Series Editor: Steven R. Martins
Book Design: Steven R. Martins

Library & Archives Canada
ISBN: 978-1-990771-18-7

ABOUT THE CÁNTARO INSTITUTE
Inheriting, Informing, Inspiring

The Cántaro Institute is a reformed evangelical organization committed to the advancement of the Christian worldview for the reformation and renewal of the church and culture.

We believe that as the Christian church returns to the fount of Scripture as her ultimate authority for all knowing and living, and wisely applies God's truth to every aspect of life, her missiological activity will result in not only the renewal of the human person but also the reformation of culture, an inevitable result when the true scope and nature of the gospel is made known and applied.

An absolutely fascinating study of an often overlooked Canadian Christian statesman and apologist. Steven R. Martins gives readers a fascinating insight into the life, work, and thinking of a man whose deep Christian commitment shaped everything he did. As Christians today grapple with how to engage politics thoughtfully and well, Steven R. Martins' book offers us a historical example whose life repays further study.

—**Andy Bannister (PhD)**
Director of Solas Centre for Public Christianity;
Adjunct speaker for RZIM;
Author of *The Atheist Who Didn't Exist: Or the Dreadful Consequences of Bad Arguments*

The study of Canada's Christian heritage has long been neglected. Few materials are available for those who desire to understand the foundational role that Christianity played in Canada's history. This publication helps to fill that void by revealing the importance of Christianity in the life of one of Canada's founders, Oliver Mowat. As Steven Martins clearly demonstrates, Mowat explicitly defended the truth of Christianity and he hoped to convince others to embrace Christ as well. Homeschooling parents and other Christian educators should find it to be especially useful.

—**Michael Wagner (PhD)**
Contributing writer at Reformed Perspective magazine;
Author of *Leaving God Behind: The Charter of Rights and Canada's Official Rejection of Christianity*

Table of Contents

Series Preface	11
Mowat: A Canadian Christian Statesman	21
Steven R. Martins	
0.1 A Canadian Profile Neglected	21
0.2 A Just Dominion	24
0.3 A Learned Province	32
0.4 An Eternal Hope	39
Christianity & its Evidences	47
Sir Oliver Mowat	
1.0 Editor's Note	47
1.1 Introduction	48
1.2 The Nature of the Christian Evidences	57
1.3 Christ a Divine Person	75
1.4 The Progress of Christianity	93
1.5 Concluding Remarks	109
1.6 Appendix	111
Christianity & its Influence	**119**
2.0 Editor's Note	119
2.1 The Spirit of the Medical Profession	119

CONTENTS

2.2 The Assumed Death of Christianity	124
2.3 The Influence of Christianity	126
2.4 The Influence of Christianity (Continued)	129
2.5 Concluding Remarks	136
About the Contributor	**141**

Series Preface

What is faith? And why should we celebrate it?

OF THE TWO QUESTIONS, the first is the most common, the second, on the other hand, is not given much thought, though it should logically follow. In our pluralistic world, the word "faith" has often been used as a token word for all forms of religious belief and expressions. You'll find it on bumper stickers, billboards, in a series of publications, even in film, music, media, you name it. Faith has somewhat become synonymous for "spirituality", which nowadays can mean almost anything. But is this *true* faith? That is, is this the true definition and understanding of faith, faith in the biblical sense of the term? The short answer is No. Not only does its definition fall short, its directional orientation is also off.

What then is faith? In order to understand what faith *is*, and what faith is *not*, we need to first understand the philosophical concepts of worldview and religion. These concepts, if based on biblical presuppositions, can help provide us with a logically consistent framework of thought, or the parameters by which we can answer these questions faithfully. Otherwise, we're faced with various conflicting definitions without any clear indication as to what is true.

Firstly, a *worldview* is what we all have, it is the lens by which we see the world and interpret its facts and evidences. There is not a single living and thinking person in the world who does not have a set of beliefs or presuppositions concerning reality. As a late apologist defined it, a "worldview" is:

> a network of presuppositions (which are not verified by the procedures of natural science) regarding reality (metaphysics), knowing (epistemology), and conduct (ethics) in terms of which every element of human experience is related and interpreted.[1]

Now, it goes without saying that not everyone's worldviews are correct. If one person believes that the earth is flat, and the other that the earth is round, and we mean in the same sense, only one of the two are right. But who? The two tests by which every worldview must be validated are the tests of logical consistency and correspondence. Is the worldview logically consistent? Does it correspond to reality? The Bible, as God's special revelation, provides us with the *true* worldview, a true set of presuppositions regarding reality, knowledge and ethics that are logically consistent and correspondent to reality. All other worldviews are antithetical to the true worldview and fail in the two tests of logical consistency and correspondence. Why? Because we live and breathe

---

[1] Gary DeMar, ed., *Pushing the Antithesis: The Apologetic Methodology of Greg L. Bahnsen* (Powder Springs, GA.: American Vision Press, 2010), 42-43.

in God's world, and thus we can also say, because of the impossibility of the contrary.

Secondly, worldviews are not free and independent from *religion*. On the contrary, our worldview and religion are inseparable. The apostle James wrote to the church that "Religion that is pure and undefiled before God, the Father, is this: to visit orphans and widows in their affliction, and to keep oneself unstained from the world" (Jas. 1:27). In other words, *true* religion is to glorify God in all that we do, in every possible aspect of creational interaction and function – this includes administering the grace of the gospel – the result of consecrating the Lord as holy in the core essence of our being (1 Pet. 3:15). But just as there is *true* religion, as defined by God's special revelation, so there is *false* religion, that which is antithetical to the truth, expressed as worship of creation instead of the Creator (Rom. 1:25). To put it simply, our worldview is the *structure* of our presuppositions, what we believe to be true concerning reality, knowledge and ethics; while our religion is the *direction* of that respective structure, our worship; it is the underlying motive rooted in the condition of the human heart.

The reason that faith has been defined and understood in various ways is because it has been interpreted and expressed from a variety of different religious worldviews, all of which place an emphasis on faith's humanistic orientation (except for the Bible). And while it might seem that some elements of their understanding of faith contain a hint of truth, they are, as a whole system, in the wrong. Having then established the parameters by which we can answer our questions, that is, from the biblical religious worldview, what can we say then to What is faith? And Why should we celebrate it?

The term "faith" in the context of biblical Christianity is used in at least two distinct senses. According to *The Oxford Dictionary of the Christian Church*, it is firstly applied objectively to "the body of truth to be found in the Creeds, in the definitions of accredited Councils, in the teachings of doctors and saints, and, above all, in the revelation contained in the Bible."[2] It is, in other words, a term used to refer to the religious worldview of Christianity. Within this 'objective' faith, there is then, secondly, the 'subjective' faith, which Paul refers to in 1 Corinthians 13:13 as one of the three theological virtues alongside hope and love. *The Oxford Dictionary* explains that this faith "is the human response to Divine truth, inculcated in the Gospels as the childlike and trusting acceptance of the Kingdom [of God] and its demands, and known as 'the faith whereby belief is reached' (*fides qua creditor*)."[3] Whereas other religious worldviews would emphasize subjective faith as a natural human act, the Bible is clear in its teaching that faith is a supernatural act, that is to say, that a Christian can only have faith as a result of God's regenerative work in his heart (Ezek. 36:26-27; Jn. 1:12-13; 3:3-8; Tit. 3:5). To put

---

2 F.L. Cross, ed., *The Oxford Dictionary of the Christian Church*, second edition (Toronto, ON.: Oxford University Press, 1974), 499.

3 Ibid.

it simply, subjective faith is a gift from God for the objective faith of God's revealed truth.

Why must faith be an external gift? Because man, in his sin, cannot of his own volition turn to God in repentance and faith. His sinful disposition prevents this (Jn. 8:34; Rom. 6:20; 2 Tim. 2:25-26; Tit. 3:3). This is not to say that man cannot choose for himself between life and death (Deut. 30:15-20), it is rather that man's will is enslaved to his sinful nature and therefore cannot choose life, the life of Jesus Christ, unless he is first freed from this enslavement (2 Chron. 6:36; Job 14:4; Prov. 20:9; Eccl. 7:20; Jer. 13:23; Jn. 6:65). He will always want to choose death, because he is hostile to the truth of God (Gen. 6:5; Jn. 8:44; Rom. 1:18; 8:7-8; Eph. 4:17-19). This deliverance from his fallen condition is ultimately the work of the Spirit of God, who takes the heart of stone and replaces it with a heart of flesh (Ezek. 36:26), and having freed him from his captivity, with his renewed heart, he is then able to choose the only logical option before him, faith in the Lord and Saviour Jesus Christ and all that that entails (Acts 11:18; 13:48; Eph. 2:8-9; Phil. 1:29; 2 Tim. 2:25-26).

This is precisely why there are so many different religious worldviews in our day and age. Sin has not only caused our alienation from God and our spiritual death, it has also affected, or we might say "infected", the totality of our being, including our intellectual, mental faculties – what theologians call the *noetic* effects of sin. Instead of interpreting God's general revelation of creation as it truly is, by our fallen and hostile nature we supress the truth and devise for ourselves false worldviews with inevitable god-substitutes (Rom. 1:18, 25). It is partly for this reason that God provided the special revelation of His word as the only authoritative interpretation of His created reality, for without it, we would be as blind men left with arms outstretched in the dark. But when God draws unto Himself men and women by his irresistible grace, these false god-substitutes are abandoned *by* faith *for* the true faith. As John Newton (1725-1807) wrote in his hymn *Amazing Grace*, "I once was lost, but now am found, was blind, but now I see."

If, therefore, faith that saves originates from God – for how else can man be saved? – then a celebration of faith is not only a celebration of what we believe, of what God has revealed – which should be celebrated in its own right – but what God has done to redeem sinful wretches such as ourselves. And what more reason do we need to celebrate faith than the fact that Christ has paid the ultimate sacrifice in order to save us from our fallen, sinful condition and the judgment that awaits the living and the dead (2 Tim. 4:1; 1 Pt. 4:5-6)? Not only does He rescue us from the darkness by forgiving us of our sin, having paid its penalty through his death (1 Cor. 6:20; Eph. 1:7; 1 Pt. 1:18-19; 1 Jn. 2:2; Rev. 5:9), He also reconciles us to the Father and begins the work of renewal and restoration, returning us, by the power of the Spirit and his sanctifying work, to our original state of righteousness and our creational purpose.

If our created purpose is, as *The Westminster Confession of Faith* states, to glorify God and delight in

Him forever (Rom. 11:36; 1 Cor. 10:31; Ps. 73:24-26; Jn. 17:22, 24), how can this at all be possible without faith? Does not the author of Hebrews write, "without faith it is impossible to please God"? (Heb. 11:6). It is for this reason also that we celebrate faith, for not only has God granted us the gift of saving faith, but faith makes it possible for us to fulfill our highest end, to glorify God and to delight in Him forever. To celebrate faith then is really to celebrate the glory of God, for true faith rooted in God's word only comes from God, the "author and finisher of our faith" (Heb. 12:2).

A Celebration of Faith is a series that reflects on the lives and contributions of those who have been touched by the grace of God, those who have professed, defended and advanced the Christian religious worldview. And while there are millions of stories to be told, the editorial team behind this series have sought to highlight some of the saints who have both inspired scores of generations towards living lives of faith, and others whose faith, although forgotten, have had a significant impact on the culture of their day. The purpose of this series is to inspire and encourage grace-bought believers towards living out their faith in such a way that demonstrates the truth, beauty and liberty of the gospel and its all-encompassing nature for the furtherance of God's kingdom.

Profiled in this volume is the nineteenth century Canadian Christian statesman Sir Oliver Mowat (1820-1903), the first premier of the province of Ontario and one of the founding fathers of Canadian Confederation. Having served multiple functions in public office during the infancy years of Ontario, Mowat is recognized in Canada's history books as a just jurist, a wise legislator, and a principled leader, a legacy which was built on the foundation of his Christian convictions. As it concerned the application of his Christian faith to public life, or exhibiting the comprehensive nature of the faith, Mowat led by example, seeking to approach every societal aspect that he was involved in as a Christian for the glory of God and the benefit of men. Towards the end of his life, as he stepped away from public office, he became a speaker for a holistic Christianity and a Christian apologist. Two of his lectures were published as books, *Christianity and its Evidences* and *Christianity and its Influence*, both of which are included in this volume, preceded by a survey of Mowat's life and his influence written by Steven R. Martins, founding director of the Cántaro Institute. Oliver Mowat, the man credited as being the architect of Ontario and a reflection of the Christian consensus of nineteenth century Canada, stands as an exemplary figure of faith, worthy of being profiled in this series.

It is our hope that the Lord may use this book to help cultivate within the church a greater appreciation for our Christian heritage, for we inherit a great treasure in the faith that we have been bought into. May you be inspired through this profile to live your faith boldly, undaunted by the challenges and afflictions of living in a fallen world, knowing that the Lord will sustain you as you seek to be the salt and light of the world (Matt. 5:13-16). And may you be equipped for, and informed as to the nature of the church's mission, to preserve and advance biblical truth, not only in its confession but in its application, for the growth of God's kingdom and for His glory alone.

May God be glorified,
The Editorial Team
Cántaro Publications

Mowat
A Canadian Christian Statesman

Steven R. Martins

0.1 A Canadian Profile Neglected

IN 1905, A MONUMENT was raised outside of the Legislative Building of Ontario, to commemorate the life of the Christian politician Sir Oliver Mowat (1820-1903). It remains to this day. However, despite being the "most famous provincial premier of the nineteenth century," as historian Donald Swainson writes, Mowat's has become a forgotten name amongst many twenty-first century Canadians.[1]

Mowat's life was one of great political achievement, largely influenced by his childhood spent learning alongside the nation's future leaders. He was born in Kingston, Ontario in 1820, the eldest son of the Scottish immigrants John Mowat and Helen Levack. He was educated in a private school in the Presbyterian tradition, alongside John A. Macdonald, the future and first Prime Minister of Canada, and John H. Cameron, a

---

1 Donald Swainson, ed., *Oliver Mowat's Ontario* (Toronto, ON.: Macmillan Company of Canada, 1972), 1.

future Member of Parliament. Mowat and Macdonald studied and worked together at a small Kingston law firm (Macdonald was five years his senior), where they also rubbed shoulders with Alexander Campbell, a future father of Confederation. It was during these early years of his public life when Mowat confessed to Campbell that he feared that he would "never be anybody," not because he desired greatness out of selfish ambition, but because he desired to be used for some significant end, a purposeful life where his gifts, skills and knowledge would be used maximally in service to God and country. Little did he know at the time that he was working with those who would unite the British provinces and form the Canadian dominion; in fact, he would himself be one of those founding fathers.[2]

Mowat was called to the bar of Upper Canada in 1841, working from the city of Toronto, where he established a profitable practice. While there he also served for two years as a member of the Toronto City Council, and as a member of the Union House, the joint government between Ontario and Quebec, until his resignation in 1864. Though not at the forefront in the confederation conferences, Mowat was nonetheless a member of the Confederation Coalition in 1864, earning the title of one of the 'Fathers of Confederation,' jousting with Macdonald about the federal-provincial relations of the Canadian dominion, and writing down

---

2 Paul Romney, "Biography: Mowat, sir Oliver, Volume XIII (1901-1910)," *Dictionary of Canadian Biography*, 1994, http://www.biographi.ca/en/bio/mowat_oliver_13E.html.

decisions of many of the conferences into judicial language.³ He also served as the vice-chancellor of Ontario until 1872, until he was persuaded by George Brown to run for the position of Premier of Ontario, which he held from 1872 to 1896. Shortly thereafter, he took on the mantle of Minister of Justice and Senator under the leadership of Wilfrid Laurier, and by 1897 accepted the lieutenant-governorship of Ontario until his death in 1903. As Swainson writes, "Mowat's public career lasted some forty-five years and was one of unparalleled success."⁴

To this day, very few books have been written on Sir Oliver Mowat. Those available mainly emphasize his public career, to the neglect of his religious convictions, but as Mowat's son-in-law, Charles R.W. Biggar, would write, we cannot understand Mowat if we do not understand his Christian faith. For example, when writing a letter to an electoral riding which had urged him to become their candidate in the provincial parliament electorate, he wrote with the utmost sincerity that "if elected, my desire is to perform my duty in Parliament in the spirit and with the views which become a Christian politician."⁵ As Biggar writes in *Sir Oliver Mowat: A*

---

3 Government of Canada, "ARCHIVED - Sir Oliver Mowat - Canadian Confederation," *Library and Archives Canada*, May 2, 2005, accessed February 1, 2017, https://www.collectionscanada.gc.ca/confederation/023001-4000.54-e.html.

4 Swainson, ed., *Oliver Mowat's Ontario*, 1-2.

5 Cited in Charles Robert Webster Biggar, *Sir Oliver Mowat: A Biographical Sketch, Vol. 1* (Toronto: Warwick Bro's & Rutter, 1905), 70.

Biographical Sketch, "there are few who would contend that the desire expressed in his concluding sentence was not sincerely felt and faithfully fulfilled."[6]

The various contributions of Mowat to the Canadian legal and political system are vast, and much can be written about them, but where the work of historians has left much unsaid about the influence of Mowat's Christian faith on his work, the man himself tells us more about this significant aspect of his life. We can best understand his work as a form of worship unto God, reflective of a life lived unto the glory of God, as he sought to realize both (i) a just dominion, and (ii) a learned province.

0.2 A Just Dominion

When Mowat first entered public office, he faced a vigorous society with a growing population and many moving pieces, whether economical, judicial, political, etc., but without much of a collective order or unity. By the end of his life he had reorganized the judicial system, codified the laws of the province, made reforms to reflect the growth of statute law, introduced employment laws, ironed out a more efficient system to administer justice, and connected cities and towns with numerous railroads for economic growth.[7] The result was the early development and ushering in of a post-Confederation Ontario, and though Mowat didn't accomplish this singlehandedly, he was essentially a chief architect of the province.

---

6 Ibid.
7 Swainson, ed., *Oliver Mowat's Ontario*, 4.

What Mowat managed to accomplish was in many ways a fulfillment of the cultural mandate of Scripture. In Genesis, man had been commissioned with cultivating God's creation into a godly civilization. Our first parents were meant to be the "royal priests in God's cosmic temple – to subdue and develop all things under God and turn creation into a God-glorifying culture," in short, bringing all things subject to the will and purpose of God.[8] Contrary to popular thought today, the world is not some social or metaphysical experiment, some blank slate for man to make of it whatever he wishes without any guiding principle, but rather, it was created and purposed by God from eternity past to be his kingdom, and the glory of that kingdom was to be developed by man subject to God in terms of God's purpose. The reformed theologian Herman Bavinck affirms this, writing:

> Gen. 1:26 teaches us that God had a purpose in creating man in His image: namely that man should *have dominion…* If now we comprehend the force of this subduing (dominion) under the term of *culture…* we can say that *culture in its broadest sense is the purpose for which God created man after his image.*[9]

This concept of "dominion" is what Mowat would have understood, and whether or not he could articulate it this way, his life's work demonstrated this reformed

---

8   Joseph Boot, *Gospel Culture: Living in God's Kingdom* (Toronto: Ezra Press, 2016), 4.
9   Herman Bavinck, "The Origin, Essence and Purpose of Man," in *Selected Shorter Works of Herman Bavinck*, ed., John Hendryx (West Linn, OR.: Monergism Books, 2015), loc. 469.

understanding of purpose and destiny. What Mowat had done, essentially, was bring about a societal structure oriented towards God. It was by no means perfect, but it was a step in the right direction. As Mowat comments regarding the Christianization of Canada:

> By the last Dominion census of Canada, 1881... out of a population of 4,324,810, only 2,634 were returned as having no religion; and nearly all the rest were returned as professing some form of Christianity... Immense progress has been made towards the Christian Ideal since Christ died on the cross; the 19th century is far in advance of the first; and is in advance of every century since... The goal unhappily is far from being reached yet; the world still abounds in selfishness and cruelty; but Christian churches, Christian societies, and Christian men and women are working for the Divine cause heartily and hopefully, never more so, in a hundred ways in all lands; and that continued progress is being made in the great work is most manifest.[10]

It was encouraging to Mowat that most of Canada was made up of professing Christians, but it was even more encouraging that the Christian religion was no privatized faith, it was the integral foundation for Canadian society. Mowat affirmed this as he wrote about the work of the kingdom of God, stating that it was the duty of every Christian to love God, and "in all respects to do God's will," for it was expected that all, regardless of vocation, were to fulfill their duties, whether civic,

---

10 Oliver Mowat, *Christianity and Some of its Evidences: An Address (1890)* (Toronto: Williamson & Company, 1890), 9, 37.

familial or ecclesiastical, as "unto God" and not to mere men (what would be coined the 'Protestant work ethic').[11] By doing this, they would be crafting the Canadian dominion into a Christian society, paying tribute to the Lordship of Christ as they cultivated a Christian culture (Ps. 72:8), and proclaiming to all the good news of salvation and Christ's righteous reign.

When surveying Mowat's work and his contributions to law and politics, it is clear that everything he did was influenced by his faith; indeed, by no other means could he have hoped to pursue a just Canadian dominion. When I refer to a 'just' dominion, I mean an awareness of justice in terms of the kingdom of God, recognizing that the state, whether federal, provincial or municipal, is accountable and subject to the Lordship of Christ, and that its function is to operate as a servant of God in faithfully administering public justice.[12] This is not the 'social justice' of our day, put forward by the cultural Marxists seeking liberation from supposed and illusory 'oppressor groups' with an infinite number of warring classes on all sides, but rather *true* justice, biblical justice, defined as God's law interpreted and applied.

This notion of biblical justice was more than mere symbolism or lip service, Mowat's life's work was devoted to this end. Although mostly operating on the provincial level, Mowat's experience and affiliations nonetheless

---

11   Ibid., 31-32.
12   Willem J. Ouweneel, *Power in Service: An Introduction to Christian Political Thought* (Jordan Station, ON.: Paideia Press, 2014), 15, 19-21.

allowed him to wield profound influence among other politicians. As historian Margaret Evans affirms, "the phrase often used of Mowat – 'Christian statesman' – is not a misnomer;" he argued, ruled, legislated and acted "with a strongly religious tone."[13] For example, when operating as a Chancery Court judge, Mowat was recognized as having reported his decisions with clarity and logical consistency, he was regarded as the high authority in the courts, and proved to be "learned in jurisprudence, skilled in technique, and familiar with precedents." It was clear to his colleagues that, as he fulfilled his duty as judge, Mowat was heavily influenced by the English Christian jurist William Blackstone, often citing his principles of the law in his deciding cases.[14] Mowat well understood the far-reaching scope of the Christian faith, and that all matters relating to justice were to be founded on Judeo-Christian values, which was the historic consensus of the pre-Confederation Canadian church.[15]

Mowat's politics were as faith-driven as his legal work, as the Rev. Principal Caven of Knox College would write concerning Mowat's moral influence in Canadian politics: "The first question he asked regarding

---

13   A. Margaret Evans, "Oliver Mowat: Nineteenth-Century Ontario Liberal," in *Oliver Mowat's Ontario*, ed. Donald Swainson (Toronto: Macmillan, 1972), 36-37.
14   Cited in Michael D. Clarke, ed., *Canada: Portraits of Faith* (Medicine Hat, AB.: Home School Legal Defence Association of Canada, 2001), 71.
15   John S. Moir, *Christianity in Canada: Historical Essays*, ed. Paul Laverdure (Yorkton, SK.: Redeemer's Voice Press, 2002), 1.

any course of action was, 'Is it right?'" It was no secret that Mowat's faith influenced all he did, and for this he was mocked by some and admired by others, but all knew Mowat's chief purpose was not personal ambition but rather faithful devotion to God. As the citizens of the Bay of Quinte District had said of him, "During your long and busy career…you always sought to promote such legislation as secured to the fullest extent the civil and religious rights of the people," and as Caven writes, "the integrity, the purity, the beneficence which we admired in his course were more than ethic virtues; they came out of the depths of his character and were Christian graces."[16]

Mowat, for example, despite his legal and political responsibilities, served as the director for the Upper Canada Bible Society, now known as the Canadian Bible Society, an organization which initially sought to distribute Bibles throughout Canada and now the world.[17] His involvement with the UCBS was illustrative of how fundamental the Christian scriptures were to his private life and public works. This is evident in his post as director of the Anti-Slavery Society, founded by George Brown, which was part of a larger international

---

16 Cited in Charles Robert Webster Biggar, *Sir Oliver Mowat, Q.C., LL.D., G.C.M.G., P.C: A Biographical Sketch*, Vol. 2 (Toronto: Warwick Bro's & Rutter Limited, 1905), 674, 691-693.

17 Julia Skikavich and Donald Swainson, "Sir Oliver Mowat," The Canadian Encyclopedia, last modified January 31, 2001, http://www.thecanadianencyclopedia.ca/en/article/sir-oliver-mowat/.

abolitionist movement. Though slavery had been in decline since 1793 in Canada, it was formally abolished in 1834 thanks to the Christian political activist William Wilberforce in England. However, the Society's attention was directed towards the United States, much of which still maintained the immoral slave trade.[18] As Mowat would comment, it was the Christian faith which promulgated laws for the protection of all persons since it was first proclaimed; laws which the pagans never truly understood or cared for. The call to end man-theft and slavery was an inevitable response to the teaching of Scripture (Ex. 21:16; Gal. 3:28), it was "the natural, necessary and immediate outcome of the teachings of Jesus."[19]

There were other ways in which Mowat demonstrated his Christian faith in public office, such as when he was approached by his electorate to find solutions for the "social ills of disease and crime." Historians have noted that with Mowat's premiership came a humanitarian movement which sought to provide comfort to the less fortunate in Canadian society. And in affirmation of the journalist Goldwin Smith's public advocacy, poverty, infirmity, and old age were declared free from being considered crimes of any sort, and that such conditions were nowhere close to warranting imprisonment. That these things were even being considered in Ontario's society is appalling to modern sensibilities, but there was

---

18   See Fred Landon, "The Anti-Slavery Society of Canada," *The Journal of Negro History* 4, no. 1 (1919).
19   Mowat, *Christianity and Some of its Evidences*, 64-65.

clearly a need to see the poor, the sick, and the elderly attended to – with some proposing not only inadequate but grossly inappropriate solutions. As Evans writes, this inevitably involved "intrusions by the state into what had been family and community matters."[20]

Historically, the church had provided healthcare, had ministered to and provided for the poor, had served and attended to the elderly. The fact that these issues were brought to the Mowat government's attention meant that the church was failing to fulfill its mission in Canadian society, for all this constituted kingdom work. In fact, one of the central concerns of pre-Confederation Protestantism was nation-building, in which humanitarian and social aid were included.[21] While the state certainly is required to protect the poor, the sick, and the elderly, to take on the role that was originally fulfilled by the church, that is to administer the grace of the gospel, was a gross violation of its biblical jurisdiction, which inevitably had significant implications for the future of Canadian society. This is how the state came to adopt the role of healthcare and welfare provider. And as a result of Canada's departure from a Christian consensus, the intrinsic moral values of caring for the sick, the elderly, and the poor are now being wrongly attributed to the humanistic worldview when historically, such 'Canadian'

---

20 A. Margaret Evans, *Sir Oliver Mowat* (Toronto: University of Toronto Press, 1992), 114-115.
21 Robert A. Wright, 'The Canadian Protestant Tradition 1914-1945', in *The Canadian Protestant Experience 1760-1990*, ed. George A. Rawlyk (Montreal & Kingston: McGill-Queen's University Press, 1990), 150-151.

values were the result of a Christian worldview (Heb. 13:16; Jas. 2:14-17; 1 Jn. 3:17). This is why Mowat's leadership, in a time when Christianity was still considered the religion of Canada, required action when very little was being done. This also entailed delivering an exhortation to the church:

> We are to bear one another's burdens, and therein fulfill the law of Christ… We are to render glad and loving service in a special sense to the friendless, the sick, the suffering and the needy… What is it that Christianity requires of us? As regards conduct towards others it requires that in every act of life each of us enquire: What does honesty require? What do justice and fair-dealing require of us? What does humanity require of us?[22]

For Mowat, the 'just' society, the 'humane' society, the 'Christian' society, were all one. It is for this reason he was credited with being a godly man whose "two chief objects of his life were the service of God and his country," as his monument outside Queens Park attests to, with the two figures of 'public justice' and 'jurisprudence' engraved.[23]

0.3 A Learned Province

It's also important to note, as we consider Mowat's achievements and shortfalls, that he was not a learned theologian. He did invest the time, outside of his private education, to study comparative religions and to learn from his father who served forty years as an elder of St.

---

22 Cited in Ibid., 115.
23 Biggar, *Sir Oliver Mowat, Vol. 2*, 688, 696.

Andrew's Presbyterian Church in Kingston. Yet because of his upbringing and public witness in politics and law, he was on occasion given opportunities to preach and teach. On one occasion, he delivered a lecture to medical students at the University of Toronto on the public influence of Christianity. This was later developed into an apologetics book titled *Christianity & Its Influence*, where he wrote:

> The average medical student, and the average medical practitioner in our province, is said to compare favourably with the average of such students and practitioners anywhere, and as regards both the learning of the profession and skill in its application. This is gratifying to all Canadians. It would be still more gratifying to all the best of them if it could also be truly said that our medical men, young and old, were distinguished above their fellows throughout the world for hearty acceptance of the Christian faith, and for Christian conduct and character.[24]

For Mowat, the role of education was vital to fulfilling man's mission as given by God. It was a necessity which, if neglected, could prevent man from faithfully and maximally serving both God and country. To him, education was more than just narrow intellectualism, it was instructing man in his mission to build God's kingdom on earth, and this involved thinking God's thoughts after him, dedicating creation unto God, and

---

24 Mowat, *Christianity & Its Influence* (Toronto: The Hunter, Rose Co., 1898), 5.

faithfully stewarding creation.[25] Mowat's understanding of the Scriptures involved seeing man's role as prophet, priest and king.[26]

We cannot dismiss the religious fervor of Mowat from his contributions to Canadian society, as several historical revisionists have done for the past fifty years, according to scholar David Yates.[27] For Mowat, the Christian faith and public office were inseparable, because the Christian faith is the only true faith. In fact, he believed that by removing the Christian faith, much of which made Canadian society a model for the international world would be lost. This concept of the Christian faith as foundational to all of life wasn't, of course, fully articulated and explained by Mowat, but the concept was evident in Mowat's thinking as a result of his biblical instruction. As he wrote in *Christianity and Some of its Evidences*, a lecture he gave to Knox Church in Woodstock, Oxford County in 1890:

> For us [Canadians] the paganism of the Greeks and Romans is nothing; for us Confucianism is nothing;

---

25 Mowat, *Christianity and Some of its Evidences*, 31-37.

26 See Cornelius Van Til, "Creation: The Education of Man - A Divinely Ordained Need," in *Foundations of Christian Education: Addressees to Christian Teachers*, ed. Dennis E. Johnson (Phillipsburg, NJ.: Presbyterian & Reformed Publishing, 1990).

27 David Yates, "'Bred in the Bone:' Egerton Ryerson, Methodist Polity and Educational Administration, 1844-1850," *Canadian Society of Church History: Historical Papers 1996*, 107, accessed February 1, 2017, http://historicalpapers.journals.yorku.ca/index.php/historicalpapers/article/viewFile/39431/35757#page=105.

Brahminism is nothing; Mohammedanism is nothing; and every other cult is nothing. If Christianity is a delusion, the whole human race is, and has been always, without a *true* religion; men know nothing of the world of spirits; nothing of the relations between God and man; the protection which religion [that is, Christianity] has heretoafter afforded to morality and order is at an end; and the whole subject of a future life is in thick darkness.[28]

Mowat's religious convictions undergirded his judicial and political contributions, and this was evident in his involvement with the development of the public education of the province. When we speak of Ontario's education system, the first person to come to mind is generally Dr. Egerton Ryerson, a Methodist minister who traveled throughout Europe on a tour to develop the Canadian education system.[29] Unfortunately for Ryerson, the Enlightenment thinking of Europe at the time was more influential in his policy-making than was his theology, as he advocated for an education system which was largely governed, determined and funded by the state.[30] Mowat, ignorant to the implications that would follow as a result of a state-run education system, was supportive of the idea, but he had a different perspective than Ryerson's.

Ryerson had adopted the Rationalists' doctrine of the mind as a 'blank slate' of potentiality, and the belief that with the aid of an educator, it could be made into

---

28 Mowat, *Christianity and Some of its Evidences*, 11.
29 David Yates, "Bred in the Bone," 105.
30 Ibid., 106.

something great. It was the "humanistic philosophy of education" derived from Horace Mann of Prussia, as the historian Bruce Curtis affirms, which essentially had no need of Christian theism.[31] The insight of a late cultural commentator is helpful for us to understand the underlying philosophy of the rationalist approach to education:

> The marvels of this [blank slate] theory for educators of the Enlightenment were immediately apparent. Man was able to remake man and the educator to play the role of a god... No modern goal in education is understandable except in terms of this hope of the Enlightenment. Education thus involved a war against the past [Christian orthodoxy] ... against which all men of intellect must make war. For the Enlightenment 'education' became a veritable mania, a magical concept which was the cure-all for all problems – social, ethical, and economic. Education would produce universal brotherhood and a paradise on earth, freedom and happiness for all... But the clean tablet concept is not concerned with education but radical re-creation of the person beyond anything envisaged by religion. It is a radically messianic and religious program, aiming at the recreation of man and his total culture.[32]

---

31 Bruce Curtis, *True Government by Choice Men? Inspection, Education and State Formation in Canada West* (Toronto: University of Toronto Press, 1992), 62.

32 Rousas J. Rushdoony, *Intellectual Schizophrenia: Culture, Crisis and Education* (Vallecito, CA: Ross House Books, 2002), 2, 7.

This would become the mainstream philosophy behind the public education system of Canada, as we witness in the present-day an attempt to redefine the family, gender, and reality; an overthrow of all Christian vestiges which initially formed the foundation of Canadian society. Ryerson had brought with him a humanistic poison, and as Canadian culture drifted over the years from the Christian faith, it moved ever closer to adopting a full-fledged, radical rationalist approach to education. Of course, because of modern education's rootless nature, it is unable to create any true 'culture' and inevitably paves the way to an implosion of itself. For how can education, steeped in secular humanism, create anything if it cannot make sense of anything?[33] How can it teach law and order, justice and the meaning of life, while rejecting Christian theism, the foundation upon which these are properly understood?

It must be said, however, that if the church had faithfully fulfilled its educational mandate, there would be little need or opportunity for the state to step in with a competing vision of education. Mowat, for example, was educated under the Rev. Robert McDowall, the pioneer Presbyterian minister of the Bay of Quinte District, who had been sent by the Dutch Reformed Church of the United States.[34] Even prior to the 1800s, schooling was provided and operated by churches and local parents in Canada.[35] However, the church gladly gave up much of

---

33 Ibid., 7.
34 Biggar, *Sir Oliver Mowat, Vol. 2*, 675.
35 Rushdoony, *Intellectual Schizophrenia*, 59.

its education mandate to the state, which at the time seemed harmless in a Canadian Christian society, but as the state became increasingly secular and humanistic, so did its education system, replacing the God of Christianity with the god of the state, collectivized man, in its curriculum.

In the end, Ryerson's Enlightenment thought, which was baptized in Christian clothing, was realized in the Canadian education system. Yet in spite of this, Mowat sought to preserve the parent and the collective church as the primary educators, so as not to hand over full authority to the state. As it concerned the development of the provincial curriculum, he followed the example of his American neighbours, who had also founded a state education system, but "was largely under local control and extensively given to religious influence."[36] Contrary to the 'blank slate' theory that was so typical of Enlightenment theories of education, Mowat believed that the mind was either in a state of covenant obedience or covenant rebellion against its Creator, consistent with the Calvinistic influence of his religious education. This is why, when establishing the Ontario Department of Education, he consulted a coalition of church leaders from the Protestant and Catholic communities to discuss the religious nature of the provincial curriculum.[37]

Prayers, Scripture readings, and biblical instruction were all introduced thanks to Mowat's work, and a vestige of this Christian influence remains today in the

---

36   Ibid.
37   Biggar, *Sir Oliver Mowat, Vol. 2*, 473-476.

Ontario Education Act, where section 264(c) states that it is the duty of every teacher to "inculcate by precept and example respect for religion and the principles of Judaeo-Christian morality and the highest regard for truth, justice, loyalty," etc.[38] It is also noteworthy to mention that Mowat had insisted that the minister of education should be a Christian minister as opposed to a candidate determined by the electorate, something which Ryerson vehemently opposed.[39] Yet in spite of Mowat's best efforts, the later displacement of the Christian religion for a more attractive secular humanism would run counter to Mowat's counsel, direction, and conviction for Canadian education.

In spite of all this, to the best of his ability, Mowat sought to cultivate a learned province, in which such learning aligned with Christian truth, for as the Synod of Toronto and Kingston stated in his day, "he showed himself to be a Catholic in the truest sense of the word, for he has always adhered loyally to the church of his fathers."[40]

0.4 An Eternal Hope

At the end of Mowat's life in 1903, many Christian Canadians began to fear the influence that Enlightenment rationalism would have on the country's society and institutions, particularly concerning the future of faith

---

38 Government of Ontario, "Education Act, R.S.O. 1990, c. E.2," Ontario, accessed February 2, 2017, https://www.ontario.ca/laws/statute/90e02#BK435.

39 Evans, *Sir Oliver Mowat*, 111-112.

40 Biggar, *Sir Oliver Mowat, Vol. 2*, 674.

in Canada. Yet prior to his passing, Mowat remained steadfast in his hope. He persevered in his belief, even on his death bed, that regardless of what turbulence might come in the years ahead to test the church's faith, the Christian religious worldview would always emerge the victor, for nothing could triumph over or negate the truth. As he wrote in exhortation to the church:

> Christians do not believe that a collapse of faith is impending; they do not believe that Christianity has received its mortal blow; they do not believe that faith in it has given way. A prophecy of the near destruction of Christianity has been often written and spoken... since Mount Calvary; but the prophecy has never come true, and Christians do not believe that it ever will.[41]

The truth of Scripture would never fade as a result of the rationalism and humanism that would creep out from the shadows (Matt. 24:35; Mk. 13:31; Lk. 21:33). Mowat knew that much, for he trusted in God's promise that God's kingdom would be made fully manifest (1 Cor. 15:24-28). Whether this first involved a time of falling away, or a steadfast persistence in covenant fidelity, was irrelevant to the end result. This was the eternal hope that drove Mowat in all his public work. As Evans writes, infused with his Christian hope, it was "under [Mowat's] careful but forward-looking guidance, that the province left behind its pioneer youth and moved

---

41 Mowat, *Christianity and Some of its Evidences*, 82.

steadily and prosperously toward maturity in the twentieth century."[42]

As we look back at this Christian statesman, we discover a devout Christian spirit which sought to instill biblical principles in all aspects of society. He was a man who walked contrary to the current of the time, for while he sought the fidelity of the church in the public square, many of the Canadian churches were headed in the opposite direction.

The gospel that Mowat proclaimed promised great transformation, which involved the fulfillment of the calling of both the church and the family. But under the sway of Enlightenment thought, the church steadily surrendered its interaction with various aspects of culture, such as education, law, arts, charity, medicine, government and more. As the Christian thinker Joe Boot writes: "We progressively retreated into a pietistic bubble, concerned largely with eternal verities and keeping souls from hell, and we faithlessly limited Christ's jurisdiction to the institutional church."[43] This cultural retreatism, which is still evident today in most Canadian Christian communities, inevitably led to the marginalization of the church and a change in the social order, for as the culture – that is, the publicly-manifested religion of the people – changed, so did the institutions. We now find ourselves in such a time where it has never

---

42 A. Margaret Evans, *"Oliver Mowat and Ontario, 1872-1896: A Study in Political Success,"* Ph.D. Thesis (Toronto: University of Toronto, 1967), 574.
43 Boot, *Gospel Culture*, 6.

been more necessary for the church to take up its plow again and recover its biblical mission, to plant and cultivate Christian education, health care services, advocacy for the protection of the unborn and the elderly, and provision and care for the poor, for all these things are essential to the church's proclamation and expansion of the kingdom of God. It is of little surprise, then, that Mowat has been forgotten in modernity, for he lived out a faith that humanistic culture loathes: a public witness of the gospel of Christ, and a model of faithful service to God in public office.

Though historical revisionists may attempt to downplay Mowat's faith and the role it played in his public life, they cannot deny the diverse testimony that credits his service to God and country. Mowat, the man of God, was the same in his private study as he was in public office. May we imitate his bold faithfulness, learn from his mistakes, and take his final words as a call to covenant fidelity and kingdom proclamation:

> As patriots and philanthropists, then, as deeply concerned for the earthly well-being of our families, our friends, our country, and our race, now and in the future; and above all, as creatures and servants of the most High God; as having, ourselves and our fellows, immortal lives to think of… and as having had communicated to us a religion of love and hope and holiness, an Atoning Saviour, a Pardoning God, a Sanctifying Holy Spirit, let us all hold fast unto the end our Christian faith, without wavering;

and let us consider one another to provoke unto love and to all good works.[44]

This profile is a revised and expanded republication of what was originally published in the EICC's Jubilee: Canada's 150th. Vol. 20, Issue: Summer (2017).

---

44 Mowat, *Christianity and Some of its Evidences*, 84.

Portrait of the Honourable Sir Oliver Mowat,
Father of Canadian Confederation,
Christian Statesman

Christianity & Its Evidences

Sir Oliver Mowat

1.0 Editor's Note

THE ADDRESS TITLED "Christianity & its Evidences" was delivered by the Honourable Sir Oliver Mowat on October 23, 1890 at Knox Church, Woodstock, Oxford County at the request of the Society of Christian Endeavor. This address was first delivered at the Breezy Hill House hotel during Mowat's holidays before it was delivered to Knox Church's congregation. It is believed by historians that Mowat's first address was slightly revised for his delivery at Knox Church, providing his hearers with a more polished presentation; he would then proceed to further revise the content of his address in order to publish it as an apologetics book under the same title, preceding his other publication *Christianity & its Influence*. While the original text of the published manuscript of 1890 has been preserved, small edits have been applied to better facilitate the modern reading experience. For example, though the original text of the chapter headers has been maintained, changes were made to the numbering of the headers for simplicity of reference. In regard to Scriptural citations, the same wording as the original citation has likewise been maintained. In addition, some footnote comments have also been added by the editor where deemed necessary for clarity, and paragraph breaks have been introduced in cases where paragraphs were running longer than a full page.

With the gradual de-Christianization of the West, and perhaps most aggressively of the nation of Canada, legacies and publications such as that of Oliver Mowat have been fading into obscurity. It is our hope that this re-publication of *Christianity & its Evidences* helps to revive an appreciation for Canada's Christian heritage and inspires a new generation of Christ-followers to live out their Christian faith by applying the gospel to every sphere of life. We trust this literary treasure unearthed from Canada's 19th century will inspire you towards living out a comprehensive, all-encompassing Christian faith.

Soli Deo Gloria

1.1 Introduction

If Christianity is true, the importance of accepting it as true is unutterably great. It claims to be a Revelation to us from the Creator and Governor of the Universe, the Supreme God; through Jesus Christ, described as the Son of God, God's only begotten Son, by whom He made the worlds and all they contain. If this claim is well founded, the acceptance of the Revelation is a matter of the highest possible duty and interest. Not to accept it would obviously be rebellion against the Almighty and the saddest of all possible mistakes which a man could make against himself, and against the loved ones whom his mistake might influence.

1.1.1 Occasion of the Lecture

In early life I studied the Evidences of Christianity very earnestly, and with all the care of which I was capable, and came to the conclusion that Christianity was no cunningly devised fable, but was very truth. In particular, Paley's *Evidences of Christianity* and Keith on the *Fulfillment of Prophecy* appeared to me to as nearly as possible demonstrate the principal positions which these authors undertook to establish. Since then much has been thought and written on both sides of the question; many anti-Christian publications for the learned and unlearned have issued from the press; and extensively circulated newspapers and magazines, on both sides of the Atlantic, contain from time to time articles or paragraphs referring to Christian doctrines in an anti-Christian spirit, or treating Christianity itself as an exploded fable. I therefore became anxious, for my own satisfaction as well as for other reasons, to consider the whole subject anew, before my intellectual faculties should begin to show diminished vigor, and with whatever advantage half a century of mental training in the discharge of judicial, professional and legislative duties may have given to me. On so momentous a subject it is most important to know as far as we can know the exact truth, and to be in a position to give a reason for our faith.

Having made some progress in this new investigation before leaving home this year for a few weeks of rest and recuperation among the mountains of New Hampshire, I took with me my books, in order that in quiet there I might continue the study. My plan in reading was, to make extracts and notes of statements and points, pro and con, which I thought deserved special remembrance or further thought. It was customary at the hotel to have an afternoon Sunday service for the guests and employees. This service was usually conducted by a distinguished clergyman from Washington, the principal of Howard University there. On the last Sabbath of my sojourn the learned doctor had been called away to preach elsewhere, and the manager requested one or other of the lay guests to assist in providing some substitute for the usual service.

After consideration, and as nothing more satisfactory could be arranged, I threw into the form of a lecture some of my extracts and notes which showed part of the Christian side of the evidential controversy; and this lecture I gave with some acceptance to the accustomed Sunday afternoon audience, in connection with a service of song conducted by others. It is this lecture, somewhat revised, and with additions since made, that I give to you to-night, at the request of the Young People's Society of Christian Endeavor.

My lecture at "Breezy Hill House," in New Hampshire, was my farewell to a pleasant place and pleasant people, never seen before. My lecture here is but an incident in happy relations which have subsisted between myself and North Oxford as representative and constituency for eighteen years, and which its people a few months ago did me the great honour of renewing for four years more.

1.1.2 Present State of Christian Belief

There never before was a time when so large a proportion of the world's population had faith in some form of Christianity as is the case now; never a time in which there were so many Christian churches; or in which the Churches had a larger membership than now; never a time in which there was more activity in Christian work; never a time in which the contributions to Christian objects at home and abroad were more liberal;[1] never a time in which there were so many true and earnest believers; and never a time in which the active defenders of Christianity were more able, more learned, more numerous, or more earnest. Among the educated classes of English-speaking Europe and America, faith in Christianity is far more general in this nineteenth century than it was in the eighteenth, and is more general today than it was fifty years ago.

I read lately in one of our Ontario journals an estimate taken from the New York Evangelist, and prepared, it was said, with much labour and care, to the effect that in the United States during the last year there had been an increase of over a million (1,089,853) church members; more than 4,800 (4,867) ministers; and more than 8,000 (8,494) churches. There has been a large increase in all these particulars in Canada also, though I have not the exact figures. By the last Dominion census of Canada, 1881, it appears that out of a population

---

1 That is to say, "more free, more expressive", not to be misunderstood with political liberalism or the decay of Judeao-Christian values today.

of 4,324,810, only 2,634 were returned as having no religion; and nearly all the rest were returned as professing some form of Christianity. I may add that I am not aware of one organized society of either agnostics or infidels in the whole Dominion, except Toronto; and I know of but one avowedly anti-Christian journal, and this journal does not pay the expenses of its production, and for want of support may soon die, as I believe some former ventures did.

But while all this is so, still beyond all doubt there are unbelievers scattered amongst Canadians everywhere, as well as among all classes of society in Europe and the United States; and among both the learned and the unlearned. No doubt some of these unbelievers here and elsewhere are so because they do not want Christianity to be true; but that is not the explanation of unbelief in all cases.[2] Some disbelieve because they honestly think, and may even regret to think, that some objections against Christianity are stronger than the arguments in its favour. Probably all of us know unbelievers who in their social relations are upright, genial and benevolent; and whose lives generally are, to human observation, as irreproachable as those of average Christians. So in classic history, we read of some non-Christians who appear, as regards conduct and spirit, to have been "almost Christians;" and there are in the present age

---

2 While Mowat does not deny the reality of man's willful suppression of the truth (Rom. 1:18) in his theology, he does however note that not everyone is conscious of this suppression, many have in fact deceived themselves into believing the lie.

writers who maintain "an adverse position towards the truth of our religion," and yet of whom so eminent a defender of Christianity as Archdeacon Farrar speaks as "men who have deepened our love for all that is great in conduct and pure in thought, and who in their stainless lives and noble utterances give the unconscious testimony of minds 'naturally Christian;'" an expression for which Tertullian is quoted. Christians must profoundly regret that such men as these have not the like precious faith in Christianity as Christians have; and that they are *natural* Christians only, or almost Christians only, and are not altogether Christians.[3]

It is proper to remember that for none of us here is the question one between the Christian religion and some other. For us the paganism of the Greeks and Romans is nothing; for us Confucianism is nothing Brahminism is nothing; Buddhism is nothing; Zoroastrianism is nothing; Mohammedanism is nothing; and every other cult is nothing. If Christianity is a delusion, the whole human race is, and has been always, without a true religion; men know nothing of the world of spirits; nothing of the relations between God and man; the protection which religion has heretofore afforded to morality and order is at an end; and the whole subject of a future life is in thick darkness.

---

3   Mowat means here people who were formed and influenced by a predominantly Christian culture but who make no profession of faith, thus they reflect some virtues in spite of their disbelief.

1.1.3 Beneficial Influences of Christianity

It is to be remembered, also, that, from even the standpoint of earth and time, faith in Christianity is not to be hastily rejected; that faith in it is in the interest of the human race as regards even this world; is in the interest of honesty, truthfulness, purity and benevolence; in the interest of all the virtues which make life happy. For Christianity adds to all other considerations for leading a good life, incentives, influences and helps of its own, and these the most powerful imaginable. Consider in this view what are some of its principal doctrines.

An all-seeing and all-observing God; a God of infinite love; an infinite and loving Saviour; immortality; a heaven, and a hell; heaven, with its gradations of blessedness, as appears from the parable of the talents and other Scriptural statements, but with blessings so great for those who love God that we are told: "Eye hath not seen nor ear heard, neither have entered into the heart of man, the things which God hath prepared for them that love him;" and hell, with its gradations of suffering, as there are gradations of wickedness, where some may receive few stripes, and some many, and where it may be much more tolerable, or less tolerable, for some than for others, but which is designated as being, for those consigned to it for punishment, a place of fire, of weeping and gnashing of teeth, of blackness and darkness – words and expressions which, whether taken figuratively or literally, or however interpreted, are well fitted to rouse sinning sleepers from their sleep, if anything could.

Independently of religious motives, it may with considerable truth be said that honesty is the best policy; that truthfulness and kindness and benevolence on our part tend to beget these qualities on the part of others towards us; that a virtuous life is happier than a life that is not virtuous; that morality is beautiful; that self-sacrifice is noble, etc. But all experience shows that without the sanctions of religion these statements have practical weight with few. Whatever value they possess is not excluded by the Christian system or by Christian doctrine; but Christianity adds to these worldly considerations others infinitely more powerful. Of these others one peculiar to Christianity is its Founder, is Jesus himself, his Person, his Life, and his Spirit, as all these are depicted in the New Testament. In Christian doctrine he is the great central truth, the great central fact, the fact of facts. Faith in his teachings; faith in his own relation to those teachings; faith in him as the truest, and best, and dearest of friends; faith that he knew all he claimed to know, and that he was and is all that the New Testament writings represent him to be; faith in him as God-man, a crucified and risen Saviour; who laid down his life for our sins, and took it again, and who still lives, and still loves; who is One with the Father, and with whom, and with the Father, those who believe, and trust, and love, and serve, may hereafter dwell everlastingly – this faith worketh by love; is fruitful in right-living and in all good works; gives "victory over the world;" and (according to evangelical doctrine) justifies, sanctifies and saves.

As a matter alike of Christian dogma and of actual experience, to love Christ is to love God the Father, and to love men everywhere, and to be ready and eager to do good. The religion of Christ is shown by experience to be adapted to every race,[4] civilized and uncivilized, and to every class and condition of men everywhere. Jesus has had, and still has, those who love and obey him amongst men in every stage both of civilization and barbarism, and in every part of the known world; amongst men of the mightiest intellect and of the lowest; amongst men of the highest culture and of the humblest; and amongst men who had previously been flagrant sinners, as well as amongst those who had always lived decent lives. Even unbelievers in him as a super-human person bow down to him as a man, for his surpassing spiritual and moral excellences, and for his surpassing genius also. Whatever they may sometimes say against the churches or their creeds, their ministers or their members, most of them have nothing to say against the great Founder of Christianity. Of him they feel constrained to declare with Pilate, "I find no fault in this man." He was the one perfect man of the human race. Christians believe that, being as Grand, and Great, and Good, and Perfect, he was more than man; that he was the Lord from Heaven. On this point I shall have more to say hereafter.

The beneficial effect of his religion on those who receive it is beyond question. It is within the personal knowledge of every observer that the best characters are made still better by it, and that many sunk in vice

---

4 Or "to every ethnicity".

and degradation have been reformed and regenerated by its influence. Examples of this abound in the history of all Churches, and of all societies established for the propagation of the Christian faith. Many such cases have occurred under the influence of the religious organizations of recent origin, as well as those of older date; of, for example, Young Men's Christian Associations (YMCA), Societies of Christian Endeavor, the Salvation Army, and the like. As to the Salvation Army, many of its officers and leaders are inferior in culture to the clergy of the various denominations, and yet they have had wonderful success; they make up for inferiority of culture by their strong faith in the Christian doctrines and their deep love for the Father and the Son. This faith and this love have in all ages been the most effective weapons, the Armstrong guns and Martini-Henry rifles, in the warfare against unrighteousness.

The question is: Can it be that this mighty power for good, which has been active for more than eighteen centuries, rests on mere fable, and must be given up?

1.2 Nature of the Christian Evidences

The evidences of Christianity are of many kinds, such as– (1) antecedent prophecies claimed to have been fulfilled in Christ and subsequent history; (2) miracles claimed to have been wrought by Christ and his Apostles; (3) the character of the teachings of Christ in connection with the life he lived, the death he died, and his resurrection from the dead, as together showing him to be Divine; (4) the general suitability of his religion to the circumstances and needs of human nature everywhere; (5) the active and successful propagation of his religion after his death under circumstances which could not have been overcome if the religion had not been true; (6) the witness of the Spirit in the heart of the individual Christian, according to the saying of Jesus as given by the Apostle John: "If any man will do His will, he shall know of the doctrine, whether it be of God, or whether I speak from myself;" and (7) some other considerations which may not come under any of these heads. I can, of course, refer to only some of these evidences, and to any but very briefly; the literature on the subject constitutes a large library, and anything like an adequate presentation of all the evidences requires many volumes. I shall select for my present statement some of those arguments which just now impress most strongly my own mind, and shall notice two or three of the principal difficulties which sometimes give uneasiness to inquirers.

It is a matter of common observation that, where there is not some familiarity with the grounds of an intelligent faith, the faith of education is apt to be disturbed, and doubts are created by objections which would otherwise have no force. It is with honest doubters, and honest unbelievers, among ordinary intelligent people, that my lecture has to do.

In these recent readings of mine I have found that, on the one hand, Christian apologists admit error in some of the positions of former apologists; and, on the other hand, some positions formerly taken by anti-Christian writers are to all intents and purposes abandoned now, and some material things in the Christian argument formerly controverted are now admitted by candid non-Christian or unorthodox critics. I shall mention to you:

Firstly, what some of those things are which unbelievers and opponents of Christianity now admit; and these an ordinary inquirer may reasonable begin his own investigation with assuming to be correct;

Secondly, I shall mention what some of the arguments are which support the facts, or alleged facts, of Christianity as a supernatural religion, and which are not so admitted.

1.2.1 What Opponents Admit

On the first point, I shall read to you at the start, as a fair summary of facts, two or three sentences from the article "Jesus Christ" in the last edition of that great work, the Encyclopaedia Britannica:[5]

> From the scanty notices of heathens even, we can derive a confirmation of the main external facts in the life of Christ, His miracles, His parables, His crucifixion, and His claim to Divine honor; the devotion, the innocence, the heroic constancy and mutual affection of His followers, and the progressive victories won by His religion in despite of overwhelming opposition, alike physical and intellectual… It is remarkable that from intensely embittered Jewish sources, we derive an absolute confirmation

---

5 This would be *The Encyclopaedia Britannica*, 8th edition published between 1853-1860, the 9th edition was not published until 1902.

of–His miracles–His crucifixion–and even of His innocence–for not a single crime but that of working miracles by magic, and claiming Divine honor, is even in these sources laid to His charge.

And again: "Even the most advanced skeptic cannot deny that by His life and teaching He has altered the entire current of human history, and has raised the standard of human morality."

I shall give you now some illustrations which I have noted of what is thus asserted, from the testimony of modern skeptics and unbelievers of eminence; and later on I shall say something of the testimony of heathens and Jews.

The great *Napoleon* was a skeptic, if not worse, as was nearly all France in his time. In his place of banishment from Europe, speaking of Christ to one of his attendants, he is reported to have made these observations:

> Between him and whoever else in the world, there is no possible term of comparison… There is between Christ and all other religions whatsoever the distance of infinity; from the first day to the last he is the same, always the same, majestic and simple, infinitely firm and infinitely gentle.

Rousseau, an infidel of the French revolution, had previously said, through a fictitious character believed to have been expressing his own sentiments: "If the life and death of Socrates are those of a sage, the life and death of Jesus are those of a God;" a God in some sense, not of course implying that Rousseau believed Jesus to be God in the Christian sense.

M. Renan, an infidel writer of the present day, whose books have been translated into English and largely circulated in Europe and America, has said these things of our Lord: "Jesus is unique in everything. Nothing can be compared to Him... The evangelical Christ is the most beautiful incarnation of God in the most beautiful of forms–which is moral man–God in man... His beauty is eternal; his reign will have no end." Jesus is "the individual who has made the species take the greatest step towards the Divine."

Strauss, the great German Deist, spoke of Jesus as the highest object we can possibly imagine with respect to religion, the being without whose presence in the mind perfect piety is impossible. Again, he said "In all those natures which were only purified by struggles and violent disruptions (think only of a Paul, an Augustine, a Luther), the shadowy color of this remains forever, and something hard and gloomy clings to them all their lives; but of this in Jesus no trace is found."

Professor Huxley, the great scientist and agnostic in a description of what he calls "the bright side of Christianity," speaks of Jesus as

> that ideal of manhood – with its strength and patience, its justice, and its pity for human frailty; its helpfulness, to the extreme of self-sacrifice; its ethical purity and nobility – which Apostles have pictured, in which armies of martyrs have placed their unshakeable faith, and whence

obscure men and women have derived the courage to rebuke Popes and Kings.

Mr. Lecky, the well-known English historian, rejects the superhuman part of Christianity, and gives, notwithstanding, this account of our Lord:

> It was reserved for Christianity to present to the world an ideal character which, through all the changes of eighteen centuries, has inspired the hearts of men with an impassioned love; has shown itself capable of acting on all ages, nations, temperaments and conditions; has been, not only the highest pattern of virtue, but the strongest incentive to its practice; and has exercised so deep an influence that it may be truly said, the simple record of three short years of active life has done more to regenerate and to soften mankind than all the disquisitions of philosophers and all the exhortations of moralists.

Again, the late *John Stuart Mills*, the author of most learned and able works on logic, political economy and other subjects, was one of the most astute of modern unbelievers in supernatural Christianity; yet, in his "Essays on Religion," published after his death, he speaks of "the beauty, and benignity, and moral greatness which so eminently distinguished the sayings and character of Christ." Again, he speaks of "the most valuable part of the effect on character which Christianity has produced" being its "holding up in a divine person a standard of excellence and a model for imitation;" that this "can never more be lost to humanity;" that "it is the God incarnate" who "has taken so great and salutary a hold on modern minds." Again:

> Whatever else may be taken away from us by rational criticism, Christ is still left, a unique figure, not more unlike his precursors than all his followers, even those who had the direct benefit of his personal teaching... About the life and sayings of Jesus there is a stamp of personal originality, combined with profundity of insight, which... must place the Prophet of Nazareth – even in the belief of those who have no belief in his inspiration – in the very first rank of men of sublime genius of whom our species can boast.

The learned writer goes on to say that in Christ "pre-eminent genius is combined with the qualities of probably the greatest moral reformer and martyr to that mission who ever existed upon earth;" and he adds that it "would not be easy for an unbeliever to find a better translation of the rule of virtue from the abstract into the concrete than to endeavor so to live that Christ would approve our life."

One more quotation to the same effect will be my last here. This is from another author, whose work, entitled *Supernatural Religion*, is probably the most elaborate and learned work of English authorship which has yet appeared against Christianity as a revealed and supernatural religion:[6]

> The teaching of Jesus carried morality to the sublimest point attained, or even attainable, by humanity. The influence of his spiritual religion has been rendered

---

[6] While not named by Mowat, the full title *Supernatural Religion: An Inquiry into the Reality of Divine Revelation* was authored by Walter Richard Cassels and published in 1874.

doubly great by the unparalleled purity and elevation of his own character. Surpassing in his sublime simplicity and earnestness the moral grandeur of Sakya Mouni (Buddha), and putting to the blush the somewhat sullied, though generally admirable, teaching of Socrates and Plato, and the whole round of Greek philosophers, he presented the rare spectacle of a life, so far as we can estimate it, uniformly noble and consistent with his lofty principles; so that the 'imitation of Christ' has become almost the final word in the preaching of his religion, and must continue to be one of the most powerful elements of its performance. His system might not be new, but it was in a high sense the perfect development of natural morality; and it was final in this respect among others, that, superseding codes of law and elaborate rules of life, it confined itself to two fundamental principles: love to God and love to man. Whilst all previous systems had merely sought to purify the stream, it demanded the purification of the fountain. It placed the evil thought on a par with the evil action. Such morality, based upon the intelligent and earnest acceptance of divine law and perfect recognition of the brotherhood of man, is the highest conceivable by humanity; and although its power and influence must augment with the increase of enlightenment, it is itself beyond development, consisting as it does of principles unlimited in their range, and inexhaustible in their application.

It is of our Jesus, and of the Religion which he founded, that all these things are said by men who, on critical grounds or because they disbelieve all miracles, do not accept Christianity as a revealed supernatural religion.

1.2.2 What Leading Facts Admitted

Call to mind here some of the leading facts which, in view of what many distinguished unbelievers have said or admitted, as well as on other grounds, may now be assumed as beyond reasonable controversy, and whether Jesus was a superhuman person or not. These admitted facts have an important bearing on the question of his claim to a Divine mission.

Jesus was certainly a historical person of the period alleged. He was a Jew. His mother and Joseph, his reputed father, were Jews. Joseph was a carpenter in humble circumstances; Jesus was born in a stable, and a manger was his cradle. His education was such as was open to the class to which he belonged, and his recorded words do not show any other human learning. He worked at the trade of a carpenter, and probably with Joseph, until about thirty years of age, when he entered on his public ministry. From that time he had no home of his own; the foxes had holes, and the birds of the air had nests, but he had nowhere to lay his head. His ministry lasted for three years, during which time he went about preaching and teaching his Gospel, and healing, somehow, all manner of sickness and all manner of disease among the people. Our Scripture record declares that from time to time "they brought unto him all sick people that were taken with diverse diseases and torments, and those which were possessed with devils, and those which were lunatic, and those that had the palsy, and he healed them."

1.2.3 Leading Characteristics of Christ

Further, this young Jew was confessedly an extraordinary and wonderful man, if he was a man, or so far as he was a man; he was wonderful for his intellectual gifts; he was a man of 'profound insight,' of 'pre-eminent' and 'sublime genius.' He was wonderful also for the lofty moral and religious standard which he inculcated, and which he exemplified in his own life – a standard far in advance of the orthodox and popular teachings of his day. He was the highest possible 'ideal of manhood;' always 'majestic and simple; infinitely firm and infinitely gentle'; unsurpassed in 'his sublime simplicity and earnestness'; a man of 'unparalleled purity and elevation of character'; whose 'life was uniformly noble and consistent with his lofty principles'; the 'grandest of all known men of the human race in all time'; 'the greatest moral reformer who ever existed on earth'; 'the individual who has made the species take the greatest step towards the Divine'; a man 'between whom and anyone else in the world there is no possible term of comparison'; 'who was unique in everything'; to whom 'nothing can be compared.' In brief: he was 'the most beautiful incarnation of God, in the most beautiful of forms;' his 'life and death were those of a God.'

It is further admitted, to be reasonably certain, that during the three years of his public life Jesus was a doer of wonders of some kind; if they are not admitted to have been miracles, they were seeming miracles; and these wonders or miracles had considerable prominence in his life. Even such an unbeliever in the superhuman as Renan, allows this much, and speaks of Jesus as a thaumaturgist or wonderworker.

The Man of whom such were the leading characteristics as practically admitted by many representative unbelievers and as depicted in the Gospels, may be described further as One who loved all good supremely and intensely; loved God the Father supremely and intensely; loved men also; and was intensely anxious that all should love God as he himself did, that all should love all good as he did, and that all should in their several places consecrate themselves to the loving service of God and the well-being of one another.

1.2.4 Some of His Personal Teachings

It was the leading purpose of Christ's earthly life, or of that portion of it of which we have a record, to instruct men as to the will of God and the way to Heaven; to make men to be in this life good, and just and merciful; beneficent and loving to one another in all the relations of life; and reverent, loving and obedient toward the Almighty God, whom he represented to be a holy God of infinite mercy and loving kindness.

Remember also that in all his teachings he spoke as having authority, "and not as the Scribes;" that he taught as if, better than Scribes or any others, he knew what the will of God was, knew the mysteries of the Kingdom of Heaven, and knew the truth on every subject to be what he taught. He recognized the sacred writings of his nation as having just authority; and, according to the Christian records, he announced that he had not come to destroy the teachings of Old Testament Scripture but to fulfill them. But he insisted that the law for men as intended by the sacred writings had been made void by traditions, to which ecclesiastical authority and popular belief wrongly ascribed an authority equal or superior to that of Scripture. The lowly carpenter denied to the traditions any authority whatsoever. He himself taught a still higher morality than Moses had taught, or was interpreted in that day as having taught; and he insisted with emphasis that this higher morality was needed in order to obtain the favour of God and the blessings of the life to come.

He further taught that God was a God to be loved by those who knew him, and to be so loved with all the heart and soul and mind and strength. He spoke of Him lovingly as Father, as his Father, and as the Father of those he addressed: "your Father." He spoke of Him as a God who loves men, all men, and not good men only. He pointed out that God causes the rain to fall on the evil and the good, on the just and the unjust. So, Peter denied his Master with cursing, and yet, repenting, he was loved and honoured to the end of life. Paul at a later period persecuted the Church, and yet, becoming a Christian, he was loved and honoured to the end by the Father and the Son. The heart of the thief on the cross had not turned to Christ until perhaps the last day of his life, but, according to our Scriptures, he then received the assurance that that night he would be with Christ in Paradise.

1.2.5 Christian Duties

Jesus taught men to live for the life to come, which is eternal, instead of living exclusively or chiefly for the life which is now, and which, with all its attractions, is short and fleeting. "Lay not up for yourselves" he said, "treasures upon earth, where moth and rust do corrupt, and where thieves break through and steal; but lay up for yourselves treasures in Heaven, whether neither moth nor rust doth corrupt, and where thieves do not break through or steal."

With this object, he taught the duty of loving God, and of in all respects doing God's will. He taught that it was the doer of God's will who would enter the Kingdom of Heaven, and that every doer of the Father's will was (touching assurance) Christ's own brother and sister and mother. The rules he gave as being the will of God for human conduct were such as these: Thou shalt love thy neighbour as thyself. All things whatsoever ye would that men should do to you, even so do ye also unto them. Love not only those who love you, but love your enemies, do good to them that hate you, bless them that curse you. He taught that we are to fulfill all our duties as unto God; and that all good done to men was accepted by God, and rewarded by Him, as if done to Himself. He taught further that the principle of duty lies in the heart, and that duty did not consist in merely outward conduct; that the heart is to be for God and goodness;

and that where the heart is far from Him, worship is in vain. Evil thoughts and desires are to be put away; evil thoughts beget evil deeds.

He further taught that without this goodness, soundness of faith was not sufficient, nor were even the possession and exercise of supernatural gifts.

> By their fruits ye shall know them. Not everyone that saith unto me "Lord, Lord", shall enter into the kingdom of heaven, but he that doeth the will of my Father which is in heaven. Many will say to me on that day: "Lord, Lord, did we not prophesy by thy name [as the revised version has it], and by thy name cast out devils, and by thy name do many mighty works?" And then will I profess unto them, "I never knew you: depart from me ye that worked iniquity."

In the account which He gave of the day of Judgment, the characteristics which distinguish the two classes of mankind were declared to be, that the one was kind "to these my brethren," and the other had shown no such kindness. Giving "to one of these my brethren" meat when he was hungry, drink when he was thirsty, hospitality when he was a stranger, clothing when he was naked, or visiting him when he was in prison – every such kindness was the same, He said, as if rendered to the Judge, even to Christ himself. "Inasmuch as you did it unto one of these my brethren, even these least, ye did it to me." Or, "Inasmuch as ye did it not to one of the least of these, ye did it not to me." To the former class would be given eternal life, and for the latter was everlasting punishment.

Such, as you know, were some of the doctrines which He taught. The effect of them on Christians was wonderful to non-Christians, and called forth from them at an early period the testimony, "How these Christians love one another."

If evil has sometimes been done, or is sometimes done still, in the name of Christianity, this has plainly been in spite of the teachings, and example, and spirit of the Master. The devil has sown his tares among the wheat; but the fields would have been all tares if no Christian wheat had been sown.

1.2.6 Common to All Churches

These teachings of our Lord and other important facts and doctrines of Christianity are common to all Protestants, and to all others professing in any manner the Christian name, including the churches between which, and our own, the differences in other respects are very great, as in the case of the Church of Rome and the Greek Church. The extent to which Protestants, Roman Catholics, and others agree was thus stated at a recent Equal Rights meeting (1st September, 1890), by so strong a Protestant as the Reverend President of the Equal Rights Association, than whom no minister of any church is held in higher honour by the Protestants of Canada:

> There is a great deal of Christian truth held in common by Protestants and Roman Catholics. Do not both Protestants and Roman Catholics believe in the moral law? And in saying that the Saviour became incarnate,

and died for us? And in the Holy Spirit our Teacher, Sanctifier, and Comforter? And in a future state of rewards and punishments? The whole range of life, and the dogmas which rule life, are common to the whole Christian world.

1.2.7 The Christian Ideal

Thus the Christian Ideal of character and conduct, as Christ set it up, and as He Himself in His own life illustrated it, is, happily, the Ideal, to a large extent, of all who call themselves Christians.

There are important differences between the churches; some of the differences being in some sense fundamental, and some being perhaps not very serious. So, within a church some earnest members may not heartily maintain all its dogmas, or concur in all its rules, or conform to all its customs. In secular matters outside the churches, there are like differences of opinion among earnest men. Differences of many kinds may continue, but, notwithstanding them all, what a world this would be if the Christian Ideal of character and conduct should be generally realized; what a world it will be when that Ideal is realized, as Christians believe that one day it will be.

Think what such a result means. All men lovers of God and of His Christ. All men loving one another as brothers love, as sisters love; and notwithstanding diversity of condition, or culture, or color, or race. No wars; no national wrongs; no hostile armies; no hostile tariffs. All men just and true in politics, in business, and in all the relations of life. No bribing or misleading of voters; no false charges against governments or oppositions; no room for true charges. No lying with type or tongue. No unfaithfulness in public or in private trusts. Rich men rich in good works. No grinding of the poor; no jealousy of the wealthy. Employers just and considerate to the employed; the employed faithful to their employers; a fair day's work receiving a fair day's wage; no strikes, and no occasion for them. No false weights or measures. No bad wares, and no bad work. No hard creditors, and no dishonest debtors. No crime, no vice. No overreaching; no cheating in a horse trade or any other trade. No one seeking an unjust advantage over another, any more than he would over his father, or his mother, or his brother. All husbands loving their wives; all wives loving their husbands; all children dutiful and affectionate to their parents. All men and women kind, charitable, courteous toward all other men and all other women. Duty the supreme affection and supreme aim of everyone.

Such a state of things is the Ideal of Christianity. It is the Kingdom of God here; the Kingdom of Heaven upon earth; and, according to Christ's doctrine, there is a still higher Heaven hereafter, where there is the ever Visible Presence of the Father and the Son. Immense progress has been made towards the Christian Ideal since Christ died on the cross; the 19th century is far in advance of the first; and is in advance of every century since the first. The goal unhappily is far from being reached yet; the world still abounds in selfishness and cruelty; but Christian Churches, Christian Societies, and

Christian men and women are working for the Divine cause heartily and hopefully, never more so, in a hundred ways in all lands; and that continued progress is being made in the great work is most manifest.

1.2.8 The End of Christ's Life and What Followed

The teachings of Jesus, His exposure of the falseness and hypocrisy of the Scribes and Pharisees, the works He did, and especially His claim to Divine authority, excited enmity and persecution on the part of the ecclesiastical authorities of His nation and others. During the greater part of his ministry he was attended from place to place by twelve of his early converts; and these during his ministry saw what he did, heard what he taught, received from him special instructions, and assisted him in his work of love. All of them belonged to his own apparent class. After a ministry of three years he was betrayed by one of these twelve, at the instance of the ecclesiastical authorities whom his teachings had offended; and, through their influence with the Roman Governor of Judea, he was arrested, and was on the same day condemned and put to death; and to the most agonizing of deaths – death by crucifixion. It is clear, further, that his apostles and other disciples believed that after being dead he came to life again; and that their faith in this was intense.

All that I have so far related respecting the life and teachings of Christ we may safely take as strictly historical facts, and as so clear and certain that they are in substance and effect admitted by candid critics who notwithstanding do not admit the supernatural element in Christianity.

1.3 Christ a Divine Person

I come now to the second part of my subject, and shall mention some of the proofs of material facts not so admitted, and some of the reasons there are for believing that this exceptional man Christ Jesus was not a mere man, but was a Divine Person, a Messenger to us from the other world, and from the Supreme God there.

1.3.1 Christ's Own Claims

Jesus himself averred this to be so, and averred it with no earthly object to gain, but the reverse. He averred that he was The Christ, and moreover, that he was in a peculiar and special sense the Son of God. That much is matter of admitted history. According to the New Testament writings, he claimed more. He claimed, for example, to be greater than the prophet Jonah, greater than Solomon, the wise and great King of Israel; greater than the temple, which was the sacred object of his nation's affection, reverence and pride. He claimed to have power to work miracles, and also to have power to forgive sins, which no prophet or priest had ever claimed to have. He claimed authority to abrogate, or declare abrogated what had been said 'by them of old time;' "Ye have heard that it hath been said... But I say unto you," etc.[7] He claimed

---

[7] This is not to be understood as interpreting Christ as an abrogator of Old Testament teaching, the law of the Lord, but rather that the authority of Jesus overturns the interpretations of men. What Jesus teaches and reveals is not only superior, but absolute.

that all power had been given to him in heaven and on earth: that all things had been delivered to him by the Father; that no man (perfectly) knoweth the Son but the Father, neither knoweth anyone the Father save the Son, and he to whomsoever the Son reveals Him. He said that he was to be the Judge of all men at the last day; that he was to come for the purpose in the clouds of heaven with power and great glory; and that he was the One who should determine the rewards and punishments due to men for their good or evil deeds.

These claims of our Lord are recorded in the Gospels of Matthew, Mark and Luke, and for the present I confine myself to these, because many unbelieving writers allow to these synoptics a reliability which they do not allow to John's Gospel. But the expressions I have quoted show that according to the three earlier gospels, as well as according to John, Jesus claimed to be a Superhuman person, and to have Superhuman power. This accords also with all that we learn from other sources.

1.3.2 His Claims Worthy of Credit

Now, that Jesus himself believed all that he averred respecting himself, I do not see how any earnest inquirer can justify doubting; and few inquirers nowadays do doubt. His perfect purity, as profoundly felt by all Christians and as acknowledged by so many eminent non-Christians, is the highest possible guarantee of the honesty of his claims. Then consider the surrounding circumstances. His claims were most distasteful to his countrymen, and to the ecclesiastical authorities of the nation; and, of all his claims, the claim that he was the Son of God, in the sense in which he knew his judges understood the claim, was to them and to all orthodox Jews the greatest of his offences. The chief priests pronounced it blasphemy; and it was for this claim that they unanimously condemned him to be "worthy of death." So it is said that in the Jewish Talmud there are tracts filled with blasphemies against Jesus, and yet that, amongst all the evil things said, there is no charge against him of any sin save his claim to be "the Son of God." John Stuart Mill, skeptic as he was, admitted "a possibility that Christ was actually what he supposed himself to be… a man charged with a special express and unique commission from God." Jesus demonstrated his belief in the claims he made, both by making them and by submitting to a horrible death in confirmation of them.

Do we need more evidence than the facts which I have mentioned supply, if we had no more to justify our acceptance of the claims made by this wonderfully pure and sober-minded teacher? This most loving, most unselfish, most self-sacrificing, this most wise and wonderful of men, so far as man he was? If we cannot accept the testimony of such a one as he was, and is admitted to have been, given under the circumstances described, whose or what testimony can we accept in regard to a matter of which men can have no personal knowledge?

But there is much more evidence of his superhuman character and divine mission than his own trustworthy affirmation.

1.3.3 Miracle of His Resurrection

Another great proof is the miracle of His resurrection. Did Christ rise from the dead after his crucifixion? It is quite certain that something or other occurred after the death of Jesus which gave to every one of his apostles for the rest of their lives intense faith in him, and supreme courage in bearing for his sake the severest toils, privations and persecutions, and the most frightful of deaths. I know of no respectable theory accounting for the course of the disciples after Christ's death, except their confident belief that Christ had really risen and was really Divine.

It is perfectly certain that the Resurrection of Jesus was from the beginning, and always afterwards, the cardinal doctrine of Christianity. Let me mention some of the considerations which show this. Nearly all the educated unbelievers of Europe who have studied the question seem to fully admit the genuineness and authority of four of Paul's epistles, even when they dispute the others. These four are the epistles to the Romans, Galatians and Corinthians; all of which were written about the year 57 or 58, or about 30 years only after the crucifixion. Now, these four epistles contain enough, without any help from the other New Testament writings, to demonstrate that the miracle of the resurrection had then the leading place in the Christian faith, was an essential part of it, was put forward as essential both as a matter of evidence and as a fact of the greatest moment otherwise. On this point let me remind you here of what is said in one of these undisputed writings of the great Apostle of the

Gentiles, the First Epistle to the Corinthians: –"I delivered unto you first of all that which I also received, how that Christ died for our sins according to the Scriptures, and that he was buried, and that he rose again the third day, according to the Scriptures," (that is according to the prophecies in the Old Testament Scriptures);

> and that he was seen of Cephas (Peter), then of the twelve. And that he was seen of about 500 brethren at once; of whom the greater part remain unto this present, but some have fallen asleep. After that he was seen of James; then of all the Apostles. And last of all he was seen of me also, as of one born out of due time... If Christ be not risen, then is our preaching vain, and your faith is also vain. Yea, and we are found false witnesses of God, because we have testified of God that he raised up Christ, whom he raised not up, if so be that the dead rise not... If Christ did not rise, your faith is vain, ye are yet in your sins... But now is Christ risen from the dead, and become the first fruits of them that slept.

All the epistles collected in the New Testament are full of the same fact or supposed fact. Every other source of information also shows that the resurrection of Jesus was from the first the universal belief of Christians; and was beyond all doubt the great and inspiring doctrine on the faith of which the Apostles and early disciples devoted their lives to the propagation of Christ's teachings, and willingly endured privations and sufferings, and often a painful death, to which the avowal of their belief subjected them.

Some of these believers had themselves seen Jesus after his resurrection, or believed that they had seen him. Others who had like faith in the Lord's resurrection had not themselves seen him after he rose, but were more or less intimate with those who testified to having seen him, and whose testimony they believed. Among those who thus believed were some men of culture and large intellect, such as Paul, and Stephen, and Apollos, and Luke.

More is known of Paul than of any other of the Apostles or early Christians. His four acknowledged writings alone are sufficient to show him to have been a man of lofty intellect. He is allowed to have also possessed all the culture of his nation and age. Before he became a Christian he had been a man of great piety, as piety was then understood among Jews of the strictest sort. He was a contemporary of Jesus, though he had not seen him before his resurrection; and he had access to all that could be said against Christianity, or against the doctrine of the resurrection of Jesus, if anything in those days could be said. He had also been deeply prejudiced against the new religion, and in favour of the Jewish, in which he had been educated, as taught and held by the chief priests and Pharisees. In consequence of his Jewish belief he was at first an active persecutor of Christians. Aftewards he became a convert to Christianity, a believer in Jesus, in his teachings, his Divine authority, his resurrection and his holy and loving character; and he became such a believer in the deepest sense. His writings, as well as all our other information, show that after his conversion, and for the remainder of his life, he was an enthusiastic lover of the crucified One, an enthusiastic promulgator of his doctrines, an untiring teacher of the Gospel of love – love to God, love to Christ, and love to men.

To this work he devoted himself with joy and boundless zeal for the remaining 30 years of his life, and therein gladly endured the loss of all earthly good, bore unspeakable suffering, and finally died a martyr's death. It is impossible under these circumstances to doubt Paul's honesty; and it is difficult to see how such a man could be deceived as to the essential facts on which was based the religion to which with so perfect a faith he devoted himself, sacrificing for its sake all earthly advantages and comforts.

The early Christians, who were not themselves personal acquaintances of Jesus, believed with equal faith, and showed the strength of their faith by the same demonstrative evidence. Among these also were some men of great intelligence, ability and culture.

It is thus perfectly certain, that the Great Miracle was believed by contemporaries of our Lord and others who had the best means of knowing or ascertaining the truth; that they believed, and avowed their belief, against every earthly motive for not believing; and that the Great Miracle was believed also by increasing numbers in the generations which followed.

If Jesus really rose from the dead, as was thus believed, nothing more can be needed to demand the acceptance of what he taught; and the only remaining question for us all is, what did he teach?

1.3.4 The Other Miracles

The resurrection of Christ, though the greatest, was not the only Christian miracle. Many miracles are claimed to have been performed by Jesus and His disciples in His lifetime, and by His Apostles afterwards. The miracles as recorded in the New Testament were of great variety; most of them were performed publicly and in the presence of foes as well as friends; and most of them were not manifestations of power merely, but were manifestations of benevolence and sympathy with human suffering as well. Their chief evidential value now is the support which they give to the crowning miracle of the resurrection of our Lord.

The great Niebuhr, described as the founder of the acutest and most independent school of historical criticism, has pointed out the totally different spirit to be found in the Gospel miracles as compared with the legends and pseudo-miracles of other religions; and has elsewhere made this statement: "The man who does not hold Christ's earthly life with all its miracles to be as properly and really historical as any event in the sphere of history, I do not consider to be a Protestant Christian." This refers to critics who argue that the Gospel story and its miracles consisted of a series of myths and legends.

The fact that, both during our Lord's life, and afterwards, he was believed both by friends and foes to have performed miracles or wonders of some like kind, is not only so recorded in the gospels, but is stated also in all other narratives of his life which appeared in the first and second centuries, and of which we have any information.

The gospels give the fullest account of these miracles, and, besides recording miracles by our Lord in his lifetime, they represent him as having given power to his Apostles to work miracles. This is the gospel record as to what he said to his disciples when he sent them forth in his lifetime to preach what they had heard from him: "Heal the sick, raise the dead, cleanse the lepers, cast out devils." In like manner, after his resurrection he is recorded to have given this promise to his disciples:

> These signs shall follow them that believe; in my name shall they cast out devils; they shall speak with new tongues; they shall take up serpents; and if they drink any deadly thing, it shall in no ways hurt them; they shall lay hands on the sick, and they shall recover.

Accordingly, it is said, in connection with the preaching of the Apostles after Christ's death: "God also bearing them witness both with signs and wonders and with divers miracles and gifts of the Holy Ghost"; "Many signs and wonders were done by the Apostles"; "By the hands of the Apostles were many signs and wonders wrought among the people."[8]

It is not supposable that these statements would have been thus made if when made it was not generally believed among Christians that miracles were then being performed, or had before been performed, agreeably to these statements. But the fact that it was so is demonstrated by Paul's admitted epistles; the fact, I mean, that miracles, or what seemed miracles and were believed to be miracles, were then well known incidents of Christian

---

8   Matt. 10:8; Mk. 16:17, 18; Heb. 2:4; Acts 4:30; 5:12

life. Thus, we have in the first epistle to the Corinthians these references to them: "To another (are given) the gifts of healing by the same Spirit; to another the working of miracles… God hath set forth in the Church–first, apostles; secondly, prophets; thirdly, teachers; the gifts of healing." Again, speaking of himself, there are these statements in the admitted epistles of the same apostle: "For I will not dare to speak of any of those things which God hath wrought by me, to make the Gentiles obedient, by word and deed, through mighty signs and wonders by the power of the Spirit of God"; "Truly the signs of an apostle were wrought among you, in all weakness, in signs and wonders and mighty deeds"; "He therefore that ministereth to you the spirit and worketh miracles among you, doeth he it by the works of the law."[9]

With respect to the miracles both of Christ Himself and His apostles and disciples there was this only known difference between Christians and non-Christians: Christians ascribed the wonders or miracles to the power of God; opponents ascribed them to magic, enchantment, satanic influence and the like.

1.3.5 Heathen Testimony

Thus, Suetonius, a heathen historian of the first century, described Christians as a "sort of men addicted to a new and *magical* superstition." Critias, a subsequent heathen author of early date, styled the Christians "*magical* or conjuring men." Origen reports of Phlegon, an

---

9   1 Cor. 12:9, 10, 11, 12, 28; Rom. 15:18, 19; Gal. 3:5

opponent of Christianity who wrote in the early part of the second century, that "in the thirteenth or fourteenth book of his chronicles he ascribed to Christ the foreknowledge of some future events… and testified that the things spoken of happened according to what he had declared." Celsus was an opponent of Christianity in the second century, and one of the ablest Christianity has had. He spoke of Christians as a "society of magicians"; spoke of Christ as having acquired his power from the Egyptians, and having on the account of them proclaimed himself God. The summary which Celsus gave of Christ's miracles shows that they were those which the gospel describes; for according to him they were of "cures, resurrections of the dead, or a few loaves which fed the multitude, many fragments being left." These wonders Celsus, like other anti-Christians, ascribed to magic and to conjurings; and he classed them with the works of magicians who, he said, professed things more wonderful than those of Christ. Heathen writers of subsequent date spoke of the Christian miracles in the same way.

1.3.6 The Jewish Admissions

The Jewish admissions are to the same effect. Here are some of them: In the tract called *Sanhedrin of the Talmud*, Jesus is said to have "wrought *magic*, seduced, and caused Israel to err." And again, it is alleged that Jesus was executed "because He dealt in *sorceries*, and seduced and instigated Israel." In the tract called *Schabbath* there is this passage referring to Jesus:

> Did not the son of Stada bring *enchantments* out of Egypt in an incision which was in his flesh… for he could not have brought them out written in a book, because the magicians examined all who departed, lest they should carry out enchantments to teach them to other nations.

So in other anti-Christian Jewish writings of the early centuries.

I do not find that any Jewish or heathen authors in the early centuries after Christ took a view as to his miracles differing from the views expressed in these extracts.

The world has outgrown the explanations thus given by non-Christians, heathen or Jewish, in the first century and several subsequent centuries of the Christian era; and the facts consequently are left with no other explanation from those centuries than the Christian explanation – the superhuman power and Divine authority of the miracle workers. No man could have done the things which they did unless God had been with him.

1.3.7 Credibility of the Miracles

Some nowadays endeavor to account for the miracles by suggesting the theory that, Christ having been an extraordinary man, and having done some extraordinary things not miraculous, miraculous acts came to be ascribed to Him after His death, and He Himself came to be adored as Divine. It is suggested in support of this theory, that Christ and the workers of miracles in His name possessed a special magnetic power, and that their laying hands on the sick and healing them was the same sort of thing as is now done by mesmerists, hypnotists and the like. But there is no historical foundation for this theory; and many of the miracles would not be accounted for by it – such as the feeding of the multitudes; quieting the storm; raising the dead; and cures effected without the presence of the sufferer, as in the case of the centurion's absent servant, and of the Syrophoenician woman's absent daughter.

The incredibility of all the miracles however established is asserted by learned unbelievers; but the mass of mankind, and of learned and cultured men as well as others, do not see the incredibility. Certainly, if we had been eye-witnesses and ear-witnesses of what is recorded in the Gospels; if we had ourselves seen Christ and His disciples performing from time to time the miracles which they are said to have frequently wrought; and, above all, if we had personal knowledge that Christ rose from the dead, and was seen by His apostles and disciples from time to time for forty days after His resurrection; that during this period He ate in their presence, conversed with them, gave them instructions as to their conduct in the future; and that in the end He was seen ascending into the heavens; if we had ourselves been eye and ear witnesses to all this, our mental constitution would not permit any of us to doubt the superhuman authority of Christ. We were not eye-witnesses or ear-witnesses; nor were we so of a multitude of other facts which, nevertheless, we believe and justly and necessarily believe.

Further: It is to be remembered that the occasion for the Christian miracles (including the resurrection) affords an adequate reason for them. Miracles are necessarily unusual and exceptional; but if we believe in a God of Providence and Power, miracles with an adequate purpose do not stand on the same footing as any others, but are as natural and fitting as other facts, and are to be accepted on like proper proofs. The purpose of the Christian miracles, in connection with the Life and Mission of Christ, was the grand one of the Redemption of the human race, a purpose which to human reason appears as important as Creation itself.

No man has a right to consider such miracles by the Great Creator as incredible.

1.3.8 Reliability of the New Testament Narratives

So far I have endeavoured to assume for the purpose of my investigation nothing material in regard to the Gospels or other New Testament writings beyond what eminent non-Christian critics have admitted in regard to them.

So pronounced a skeptic as Rousseau has said that "the Gospel has characteristics of truthfulness so striking, so perfectly inimitable, that its inventor would have been more astonishing than its hero."

In like manner John Stuart Mill has said:

> It is of no use to say that Christ as exhibited in the Gospels is not historical, and that we know not how much of what is admirable has been superadded by the tradition of his followers... Who among His disciples or among their proselytes was capable of inventing the sayings ascribed to Jesus? Or of imagining the life and character revealed

in the Gospel? Certainly not the fishermen of Galilee. As certainly not St. Paul, whose character and idiosyncrasies were of a totally different sort. Still less the early Christian writers, in whom nothing is more evident than that the good that was in them was all derived, as they always professed that it was, from the higher source.

Renan has this statement:

It is sufficient for me to say that the more I reflected, the more I have been led to believe that the four books recognized as canonical bring us very near the age of Christ; if not in their last revision, yet at least in regard to the documents that compose them… I admit the four canonical Gospels as serious documents. St. Matthew evidently deserves peculiar confidence for the discourses. Here are the oracles, the very notes taken while the memory of the instruction of Jesus was living and definite… Mark, the most ancient, the most original, and to which the least of later additions have been made… He is full of minute observations, proceeding beyond doubt from an eye-witness. There is nothing to conflict with the supposition that this eye-witness, who had evidently followed Jesus, who had loved Him and watched Him in close intimacy, and who had preserved a livid image of Him, was the Apostle Peter himself, as Papias has it… As to Luke, doubt is scarcely possible… The author is certainly the same as the author of the Acts of the Apostles. Luke's Gospel was written not long after the siege of Jerusalem, and it is extremely probable that Luke was a disciple of Paul.

Strauss has this statement:

> The review of evidence with regard to the first three Gospels gives this result, that soon after the beginning of the second century [that is the time he names] certain traces are found of their existence, not indeed [he alleges] in their present form, but still of the presence of a considerable portion of their contents, and with every indication that the source of these contents is derived from the country which was the theatre of the events in question.

Other quotations to the same effect might be added from other writings holding the same position as these toward Christianity.

The observations which I have just quoted were not intended to apply to the Resurrection or other miracles as recorded in the New Testament writings, nor the details there given of them. These details, if correct, are important as showing that neither the resurrection nor the other miracles can be reasonably explained away. It is from the New Testament writings alone that we obtain direct evidence for such details.

As to the Resurrection, for example, it is from the Gospels and Acts we learn that Christ was not only seen by the witnesses named, but repeatedly ate with His disciples; that when His appearance frightened them, and they thought it was or might be, not Christ whom they saw, but a spirit, He told them (in the voice they knew and loved so well) to handle Him, as (He said) a spirit had not flesh or bones as He had; and that on repeated occasions He showed them his hands, and His feet, and His side; the hands and feet which has been pierced with the nails that bound Him to the cross, and the side which had been pierced with a soldier's spear in order to make sure that He was dead.

So it is from the New Testament writings we learn that Jesus spoke to the disciples from time to time during 40 days after His resurrection; that He spoke to them concerning the Kingdom of God; now reproving them for the weakness of their faith; now giving them encouragement, and now instruction; showing them from the Old Testament Scriptures that the Christ should rise from the dead the third day as He had risen, and that repentance and remission of sins should be preached in His name unto all the nations, beginning at Jerusalem; and that He further prepared them, by the promise of miraculous gifts and otherwise, for the work of preaching the gospel to all the world, and making disciples of all nations.

These and other details could be no illusion even if mere appearances of Christ, without words spoken or bodily acts done, might be illusions. Why are not these details to be believed? If the other parts of the Gospel narratives are found or admitted to be at least substantially accurate, why are not the supernatural parts also to be taken to be correct?

It is admitted that the Gospels in their present form, including what they narrate as to the resurrection and other miracles, were in use as early, at all events, as the latter half of the second century, and that these

Gospels had then a sacred authority among Christians and Christian societies generally. Christian critics hold the Gospels to have been originally in the same form as now, and hold the three earliest, Matthew, Mark and Luke, to have been written and in use several years before the destruction of Jerusalem by Titus in 69 or 70. Opponents admit that they were in existence about that time in some form, but do not admit that they were the same then as now. I have already pointed out that the fact of the Resurrection was asserted and believed from the very first; and I have mentioned some of the reasons why the miracles recorded in the New Testament are to be believed.

In connection with these observations, three things are to be noted with reference to the narratives which the Gospels and Acts contain of the resurrection and other miracles: (1) These narratives fit in naturally with the context, and the miracles are frequently the occasion of some of the Saviour's most striking and characteristic sayings. (2) It is admitted that the miracles with their details were believed before the middle of the second century, and that, say, by the year 180 the narratives containing them were in the form in which we have them now. (3) On the other hand, there is no evidence that the narratives ever existed without the miracles; no evidence of the details of these having ever been given differently; no evidence that these details as we now have them were not believed from the first; and no evidence of any counter tradition in regard to them amongst anti-Christians, whether Jewish or Pagan. On this last point it is to be remembered that the unbelieving Jews were always more numerous than the Christian Jews, and that there was always the fiercest antagonism between them. The absence of any counter tradition regarding either the fact of the miracles or the details of the miracles, is thus of great weight.

In brief, there appears to be so much evidence in favour of the Gospels and Acts as a whole, miracles and all, that no man can safely or justifiably, in a matter so momentous, refuse to accept these writings as giving throughout a true statement, or a substantially true statement, of the events recorded, viz: of the life and teachings, the miracles and Resurrection, of the great Founder of Christianity. In the evidences, or in some of the doctrines taught, there may to some minds be difficulties; but in the rejection of Christianity and its records, there are difficulties greater still; and in such rejection there is grave danger, as well as these difficulties.

1.4 The Progress of Christianity

A further weighty argument for Christianity is founded on the wonderful progress which the religion made in the first and second centuries, and has continued to make. It has for many centuries been the religion of the civilized world. Nor has it been accepted as matter of mere form. It is really and truly believed in by the great majority of the people of Christian nations, and of the most gifted men and women as regards intellectual endowment, as well as of those least gifted. Many millions in the last nineteen centuries have earnestly striven to make Christianity as they understood it the guide of their lives; and many other millions have believed it and made no such effort, but have been more or less restrained and otherwise influenced by their belief in it. Thousands and thousands, including persons of all races and classes, have willingly died for their faith in this religion, and I am sure there are now thousands in every part of Christendom who, if called on, would willingly die for its sake.

Christianity is the great power for good in the civilized world. But it had mighty obstacles to overcome, and especially in the early centuries. It was hateful to the great body of the Jews. Outside of Judea, it was despised as coming from a despised nation. It was hateful to the great majority of the Gentiles everywhere. Paganism was no restraint on man's selfishness or sins. On the contrary, it encouraged all manner of lawlessness and indecency. In Romans 1:24 and following verses, St. Paul described some of the practices which flourished under it. Heathenism had even its gods for assisting the commission of crime and indulgence in vice. A thief had a god to whom he might hopefully pray for success in his thieving enterprises. A man impatient for the death of a relative whose property he expected to inherit, had a god to whom he might pray to expedite the death he desired. Far worse things than even these characterized Roman belief and Roman manners, as well as the beliefs and manners of other peoples, in and before our Saviour's time, and thenceforward until Christianity acquired sway among the nations.

But Christianity from the earliest days of its appearance in the world began to introduce its beneficence, its morality, and its spirit. The first recorded organization of Christians was for the better distribution of charity to those in need; and among the first results of the political triumph of Christianity in the Roman Empire, was the promulgation of laws for the protection of children and slaves, and laws regulating in a more Christian spirit the relation of the sexes. The moral influence of Christianity was further shown in its having from the earliest time promoted a purer literature, a higher moral life, and a better public spirit than had previously existed; and in the establishment at a very early period of buildings for the reception of strangers, almshouses for the poor, hospitals for the sick, orphan houses for the forsaken, and houses of refuge for helpless old women and men. These were new institutions, which paganism, and pagans in general however cultured, had known nothing of and cared nothing for. But benevolent institutions and beneficent acts of every description are the natural and necessary and immediate outcome of the teachings of Jesus.

It has been said and I apprehend justly said, that of the efforts which in the history of the past have been made for the improvement of mankind and the self-sacrifice which these efforts have evoked, nine-tenths, and perhaps 99 per cent, have been called forth by Christianity; by the teachings of Jesus, and by regard for Him, His Person and His Work.

Christianity is a religion of self-denial, a religion which forbids many things to which human nature is inclined, and requires many things to which human nature is disinclined. To most men in every age it is for this reason not an agreeable religion to accept, and unless believed to be true is not likely under ordinary circumstances to be accepted. Besides this, in Christ's own time, and for nearly three centuries afterwards, a confession of faith in him involved earthly sacrifices of every kind, and sufferings, even at times to the death, and the most excruciating and terrible of deaths. It was in spite of all these obstacles and difficulties that the religion of the young Jewish carpenter spread immediately after His death, and with an ever-increasing activity, through every part of the known world; became in less than three centuries the national religion of the Roman Empire, then comprising almost the whole known world; and went on spreading; and is now, and for centuries has been, in some form, the religion of the most civilized and most cultured nations of the world.

Let us ask ourselves here: Who was the founder of the wonderful religion which accomplished such mighty results against such enormous obstacles and difficulties? Humanly speaking, he was a young Jewish village carpenter, born in Bethlehem and brought up in Nazareth, obscure villages of Judea, a conquered Province of the Roman Empire, who had been put to death by the Roman Governor as a malefactor. How could such a man create a religion like Christianity, in such a state of the world as then existed? How could such a religion, if there was no supernatural element in it, have become, after the founder's death and by the year 313, the religion of the great Roman Empire, then at the height of its civilization and greatness and power? And the religion for all the centuries since of the most civilized parts of the civilized world?

How could a religious system, thought out by an obscure Jewish carpenter, taught by His mouth for but three years, and distasteful to the masses and to their governors and priests, become, if there was nothing superhuman about it, the greatest power ever since in influencing the institutions, and laws, and government, and practical life of the nations? If this religion was from God, and attested from the first by due proofs, its progress contains no wonder. But otherwise, nothing surely to human reason could be more hopeless than the chance of such a future, nothing more out of the question, when the young carpenter was put to death by the Roman Governor. If He wrought no miracle, if He did not rise from the dead, if He was a mere man, without superhuman intelligence, power or mission, the progress which His religion made after His death is a greater wonder than the wonders which Christians believe that He wrought by superhuman power.

Did the new religion owe its wonderful propagation, not to Jesus Himself, but to its having been taken up after the death of the teacher by the eleven disciples who remained after the treason and suicide of Judas? Nowadays it is not pretended that they were imposters, or in any sense bad men, or had any earthly object to gain by what they did; quite the contrary. What power had they to spread the religion of the crucified Jesus, if there was nothing superhuman about it? As Jews they were despised by all others; and they were Jews of humble position and attainments. Not one was a man of education. Not one supposes that any of them had the intellect or moral force of Jesus Himself. Not one had remarkable ability of any kind, not to speak of ability for so mighty and exceptional an undertaking.

They had in the three years of the public life of Jesus been a good deal with Him, had formed considerable attachment to Him, and had faith in His teachings; but they understood many of His teachings wrongly; and they had not expected Him to be put to death, or to rise again. One of them so little expected His resurrection, and was so incredulous in regard to it that, when others told him that the body of Jesus was no longer in the tomb, and that they had seen Him alive, he said he would never believe unless he should himself see in the hands of the supposed Jesus the print of the nails, and put his own finger into the print of the nails, and put his own hand into the pierced side of his Lord. The faith of all the disciples up to the time of Christ's death is recorded to have been imperfect and weak. Not one had faith and courage enough to remain with Him in His extremity. When the soldiers came to arrest the Lord, the first impulse of the impulsive Peter was to fight. That Jesus did not permit; and when immediately afterwards Jesus was seized and bound by the soldiers, all the disciples who were then with Him forsook Him and fled. Peter and one other disciple followed when He was led away, but they followed afar off. Having got into the court to which Jesus had been taken, Peter, in conversation there with other bystanders and in the very presence and sight of the Lord, denied repeatedly, and the last time with an oath, that he was a disciple of His, or even knew Him. We hear of no other disciple approaching Him, even at a distance, until after He had been nailed to the terrible cross. Were these such men that, without any miracle having been performed, and without any superhuman authority or strength, could impose on the world the religion of the crucified Jewish carpenter?

Everything was against such an undertaking; the religion was hateful to all but the few hundred persons who had become in some sense the disciples of Jesus during His life; His crucifixion as a malefactor was to the Jews generally a stumbling block, and made the new religion seem to the Gentiles utter foolishness. Except the superhuman character of our Lord, the superhuman works which He had done, and had empowered His disciples to do, and His Resurrection from the dead, the disciples had nothing to go upon, either for their own encouragement or for bringing others to believe. If Jesus had not risen from the dead, and if He had done no work of supernatural power, and if they had themselves no such power, how could they possibly have succeeded in convincing the world that His religion was Divine? Or how could they have had the courage, or the desire, to make the attempt? Their success under such circumstances would be a wonder as great as the Resurrection of the crucified Christ, or as the other miracles which are recorded to have been wrought.

It is far easier to account for the wonderful progress of Christianity in the early centuries on the supposition that the miracles and other facts set forth in the New Testament are true, than on any other theory. Christians believe that they are true.

1.4.1 Lessons for those who still Doubt

That the considerations which I have been stating, whether absolutely conclusive or not, have at all events some substantial force, is undeniable. Honest unbelievers are not always familiar with them, or with the other evidences of Christianity, and their unbelief sometimes arises from that cause. Other honest unbelievers think that, strong though the argument may be from these considerations and others, there are grounds for disbelief in the circumstance of the evidences of Christianity not being still stronger and clearer and more free from difficulty than they are. Such persons cannot believe, or some of them cannot believe, that if Christianity were true, God would not have made the evidences of it certain, and not merely more or less probable; and they think that the evidences are at the most probable only.

As to believing in Christianity on probable evidence only, we all know that in the case of many or most other matters of importance in this world, things are so constituted (whatever the reason may be) that we have to act, and do constantly act, on probable evidence only;

and it is surely therefore the height of unwisdom for anyone to reject Christianity because in his judgment the evidence does not demonstrate its truth, or because there may not be in its favour the kind or degree of evidence which he would like or would expect. How many opinions on worldly matters do we all hold firmly, and are wise in holding, though their truth, as we know, is not demonstrable, and may be very far from being demonstrable? Almost every question of politics, or legislation, or business, and every step in life needing consideration, we have to decide, and do decide, on probability only, or on what on the whole may seem the probability. Further: we know that many things are true though they cannot be proved at all; and that many things are true though surrounded by the greatest improbabilities. We have no ground asserting that this may not be so in the case of religious evidences also.

Again, some honestly disbelieve or doubt, because it is contrary to their notions of God that there should be suffering in the next world, or so much of it; or that if a way of escaping exists or is provided, as Christianity teaches, all men should not have been made more acquainted with that way, and all men made by the power of God or otherwise to avail themselves of it.

Most of those who seem influenced by either of these objections are not atheists. Atheists nowadays constitute a very small portion of those who, living in Christendom, are not believers in some form of religion. Most unbelievers consider, as Christians do, that the universe was not self-created, and was not the result of blind chance. They believe, that there is, certainly or probably, a great First Cause, a Personal God, self-existent and eternal, the Creator and Governor of all worlds, and that He is a Being of great Goodness, and of transcendent Power, and Knowledge, and Wisdom. To any who so believe, the objections to Christianity ought to make no difficulty as against the evidences in its favour, for, as John Stuart Mill has testified, "the Christian religion is open to NO objections, either moral or intellectual, which do not apply to the common theory of deism."

As to both grounds of doubt or disbelief which I have mentioned, it is ever to be borne in mind that, apart from Revelation,[10] nothing whatever is known of the next world except what may be logically inferred from matters in this world; that the earth is but a speck of creation; and that God's moral government may have reference to a million of worlds, and to time without end. As against Revelation, or an asserted Revelation, how can we suppose ourselves competent to say, from our little standpoint, and with our limitless ignorance, what are or are not the moral needs and necessities of the Eternal Universe, as these are known to its Creator, and omniscient Governor? How could any one of us justify rejecting Revelation on the ground that its teachings as to a future life do not accord with the speculations and guesses which he may choose or may have chosen to indulge in?

---

10 By "Revelation", Mowat means by God's creational and special (written) revelation.

In this instance the Christian doctrine is supported by the analogy of the earthly things which we know something about; for we know from our own personal experience and observation, that there is much suffering in this world, whatever there may be in the next; that there is suffering here in many forms affecting man, affecting even infants of the tenderest age, and affecting the lower creation also; that the sufferings of the human race are of all kinds, mental and physical, and sometimes are terribly severe, and sometimes last as long as life. We know also that there is in this world no end of vice and crime and cruelty. We know further that there are practical modes of avoiding much of the suffering, that these modes are not known to all sufferers, and that many suffer on from want of knowledge which others may possess. We know also that there have always been great diversities in the conditions of men in this world as respects such suffering, and as respects comfort and happiness generally.

What does this state of things show? It shows to a demonstration that, whatever the reason may be, the constitution of the universe is certainly such, that suffering and the sufferer's ignorance of remedies are not inconsistent with the Power and other Attributes which belong to the Supreme Governor of all things, and are not inconsistent with the perfect wisdom and benevolence which are ascribed to Him both by Christians and by most non-Christians who live in Christian lands. The full explanations which would enable us to clearly see the reason and to clearly perceive the consistency, have not hitherto been revealed, and may require (and I dare say do require) other faculties than we now have to understand or fully appreciate them. But if there is certainly much suffering in this life, the fact is material in considering what is revealed as to this life. Revelation, if we believe it, gives us some insight into the spiritual world, but beyond what we may thus learn there is utter darkness.

In reference to suffering in the next world, as revealed in the Scriptures, Bishop Butler in his great work has these observations:

> All shadow of injustice, and indeed all harsh appearances in the economy of Providence, would be lost if we would keep in mind that every merciful allowance shall be made, and that no more will be required of any one than what might equitably be expected of him from the circumstances in which he was placed, and not what might have been expected had he been placed under other circumstances; that is, in Scripture language, that every man shall be accepted according to what he had, not according to what he had not.

The rules of this moral government are not rules of ignorant, weak and sinful man's devising, but are rules of which the all-knowing, all-just, all-holy and all-wise God is the author. Let none of us deceive himself with a false hope of safety, or trust his eternal life to what a sin-loving heart may suggest; instead of earnestly and gratefully accepting the teachings of the God-man, the Lord from Heaven.

1.4.2 Lessons for those who still Doubt (Continued)

One consideration more on the general question. It is a certain fact that from a period antecedent to Christianity's becoming the national religion of the Roman Empire up to the present time, the immense majority of the world's thinkers have deemed the evidences of Christianity as a supernatural religion to be sufficient to establish its character in that respect, notwithstanding all the difficulties and objections which have from time to time been urged with more or less force; and these men have felt themselves able to accept the religion as true, and with all their hearts to receive and hold it as Divine. Amongst these great thinkers have been such grand men in intellectual attainment as Paul of Tarsus in Apostolic times; as Justin, Tertullian, Origen, Athanasius and Augustine, in the early centuries; as Liebnitz, Descartes, Haller, Copernicus, Kepler, Bacon, Newton, Cuvier, Ray, Brewster, Faraday and Agasiz, amongst scientists who have passed away; as Mr. Mivart, Sir William Thomson, and Professor Stokes, amongst modern physicists; as Niebuhr, the great historian of whom I have already spoken; as Sir Matthew Hale, Lord Cairns and Lord Selburne (not to name others) amongst eminent English judges; as Mr. Gladstone, a profound and successful seeker after truth in many fields; as our own Sir Daniel Wilson and Sir William Dawson, both of whom have a world-wide fame in their several departments of science and learning, and are at the same time among the most earnest and active of Christians; and as a host of other able and learned scientists, philosophers, historians, judges, legislators, literary men and theologians, of the highest distinction, in all countries and ages. That the evidences have been sufficient thus to satisfy the great majority of cultured thinking men for many centuries show that there must be a good deal in those evidences, and more than an earnest inquirer can safely disregard.

Again: if, as against the evidences and arguments in favour of Christianity, the most that an agnostic or a skeptic can say is, that the evidences are not sufficient to demonstrate the truth of Christianity, or that in his judgment the probabilities are outweighed by improbabilities in the evidences or the doctrines, his position implies the at least possible truth of Christianity. Indeed, the name which unbelievers now prefer to all others, is "agnostics," or persons who disclaim actual knowledge. But if Christianity is true, it is of unspeakable importance, with reference both to an eternal life after death and to the good of the race in this world, that Christianity should be accepted; while if not true, there is on the one hand at least no harm in accepting it heartily and unreservedly, and on the other hand there is, beyond all doubt as regards this life, much good. If, therefore, Christianity is even possibly true, common sense and prudence and philanthropy alike require its acceptance, notwithstanding arguments against it which, however strong they may seem to any, leave its truth to be a possibility. In all other affairs, prudent and sensible men so act, and in other affairs the sake is infinitely less than in this matter of the Christian religion.

If, notwithstanding these considerations and others which bear in the same direction, an honest inquirer here or elsewhere finds that the evidences which have satisfied the great majority of learned thinkers for many ages fail to satisfy his understanding, and if he looks upon some of the arguments against Christianity as overwhelmingly stronger than the arguments for it, why should he endeavour to impress this opinion on others? Why should he want to lessen the wonderful Teacher's influence in the world for good? If he is a lover of his race, why, doubt as he may the logical sufficiency of the evidences, should he not, in spite of his doubts, take the side of the wise and loving Jesus, in the work of good for which He laid down His life? Why should he join any hostile camp? Why, on the contrary, and notwithstanding logical and other difficulties if he has these, should he not leave to those who believe the undisturbed use of Christianity for the beneficent work of advancing right living and consequent happiness in the world?

Very few can persuade themselves that the race would not suffer, and suffer unspeakably, by the blotting out of the religion of Christ. A distinguished writer among ourselves, one of Tertullian's "natural Christians," has published eloquent words of anxiety and warning to those who think with him that a "collapse of faith" is at hand, that as the result of science and criticism combined "belief in Christianity as a revealed and supernatural religion has given way," has received a "mortal blow." I shall read to you an extract from his words of warning:

What then is likely to be the effect of this revolution on morality? ...What will become of the brotherhood of men and of the very idea of humanity? Historically these beliefs are evidently Christian. Will they survive the doctrines with which in the Christian creed they are inseparably connected of the universal fatherhood of God, and of the fraternal relation of all men to Christ? "God" says the New Testament, "hath made of one blood all nations of men for to dwell on all the face of the earth." Blot out the name of the Creator, and on what does this assertion of the unity and virtual equality of mankind rest? What principle forbids the stronger races[11] or those that have superior firearms to prey upon the weaker? What guards the sanctity of human life, if there is nothing more divine in man than in any other animal?

May we not add: What in the absence of Christianity would guard anything which is distasteful to the natural heart, or stands in the way of a man's desires? But Christians do not believe that a collapse of faith is impending; they do not believe that Christianity has received its mortal blow; they do not believe that faith in it has given way. A prophecy of the near destruction of Christianity has been often written and often spoken, with more or less seeming reason, since the founder of Christianity was crucified on Mount Calvary; but the prophecy has never come true, and Christians do not believe that it ever will.

---

11 As expressed in the context of the citation, "races" here does not presuppose polygenesis, but rather what is meant is "ethnicities" or peoples of different nations.

The sciences may have shown errors in some former interpretation of portions of the Old Testament. Criticism may have corrected other popular errors in the case of both Testaments. It is right and desirable that errors should be corrected;[12] all intelligent Christians so hold. But as regards the essential facts and essential doctrines of Christianity, Christians perceive nothing to fear from either science or criticism. The great majority of the ablest and most learned scientists and critics have been Christians. In the full light of science and criticism, Christianity, of all beliefs positive or negative, continues to be, in the general judgment, the best belief to live in, and the safest belief to die in.

1.5 Concluding Remarks

In view of the whole subject, I trust I may say with all sincerity for myself, I know I may say for many of you, I wish I might say for all, that in the great battle of Religion and Morality we and all ours take the side of the Man of Nazareth. The history of the world has presented no leader like Him. He is the only leader worth a thought. We gladly take Him for our Leader, and for our King, our Master, our Example, our Guide. We gladly recognize Him as God-man, a Messenger from Heaven, the Redeemer of the world. Believing what the New Testament tells of Him, we love Him dearly. In the light of His teachings, we mourn over the imperfections

---

12 *Human* errors, not once does Mowat claim that the written revelation of God contains any errors, but rather the fault, if any, can only fall on man's interpetations.

and shortcomings and sins of our lives. It is our earnest desire that (God helping us) we and all ours should be like Christ, should possess His spirit, should be doers of the Father's will, and should be able to live and die in the blessed hope that after our earthly lives are over we shall be forever with the Lord who bought us, and with those who on earth are dear to us, as we know or believe they are dear to Him.

As patriots and philanthropists, then, as deeply concerned for the earthly well-being of our families, our friends, our country, and our race, now and in the future; and above all, as creatures and servants of the Most High God; as having, ourselves and our fellows, immortal lives to think of, and (if we can) to provide for; and as having had communicated to us a Religion of love and hope and holiness, an Atoning Saviour, a Pardoning God, a Sanctifying Holy Spirit, let us all hold fast unto the end our Christian Faith, without wavering; and let us consider one another to provoke unto love and to all good works.

1.6 Appendix

Comments on *1.1.2 Present State of Christian Belief*:

In further illustration of what is said in the lecture as to the present condition of religious belief, the following extracts from the *North American Review* for July 1885, with respect to the United States, are interesting:

> "In the time of Aaron Burr," says Parton, "it was confidently predicted that Christianity could not survive two more generations." Of the same period another writer states that, "wild and vague expectations were everywhere entertained, especially among the young, of a new order of things about to commence in which Christianity would be laid aside as an obsolete system." Considerably more than a century ago Voltaire said: "Before the beginning of the 19th century Christianity will have disappeared from the earth." It is an instructive coincidence that the room in which Voltaire uttered these words has since been used as a Bible repositary.

Comments on *1.2.7 The Christian Ideal*:

The following are extracts from the same source, the *North American Review* for July 1885:

> In the year 1800 there were in the United States 3,030 evangelical churches; in 1850, 43,072; in 1870, 70,148; and in 1880, 97,090; a gain of 27,000 in ten years, ending in 1880. ...As gleaned from the "year-books" and "church minutes", the number of communicants in evangelical churches in the United States has been

as follows: In 1800, 364,000; in 1850, 3,529,000; in 1870, 6,673,000; and in 1880, 10,065,000. Of course during all this time there was an immense increase in population, but the increase in church membership a good deal more than kept pace with that of population. Taking the whole country through, there was in 1800 one evangelical communicant to every 14.5 inhabitants; in 1850, one to every 6.5; in 1870, one to every 5.75; and in 1880, one to every 5. Even during the period since 1850, in which materialism and rationalism have been subjecting Protestantism to so severe a strain, while the increase in population has been 116%, the increase in communicants of Protestant evangelical churches in the United States has been 185%.

The same pronounced drift Christianwards evinces itself if we consider the matter of American colleges and college students. Writing in 1810, Bishop Meade, of Virginia, said: "I can truly say that in every educated young man in Virginia whom I met I expected to find a skeptic, if not an avowed infidel." When Dr. Dwight became president of Yale Colleges in 1745, only five of the students were church members. In the early part of Dr. Appleton's presidency of Bowdoin, only one student was a professing Christian. In 1830, according to returns obtained from American colleges, 26% of the students were professing Christians; in 1850, 38%; in 1865, 46%; and in 1880, according to the year-book of the Young Men's Christian Association, out of 12,063 students in 65 colleges, 6,081, or a little more than half, were professors of religion…

Christianity & Its Evidences | 113

So far from Christianity betraying the first symptoms of exhaustion, there has been no time since the Jordan baptism of Jesus when Christianity has moved with such gigantic strides and put forth efforts so vigorous and herculean, as during these years of our own century when the disciples of Voltaire and the imitators of Paine have been most active... It is during this time, in fact within the last forty years of it, that there have sprung up all our Young Men's Christian Associations, with organizations extending north and south, east and west, in North America and South, Europe, Asia, the Sandwich Islands, Australia, Madagascar. ...Our American Sunday schools, too, are all of them a growth of the present century, numbering only half a million pupils in 1830, with an increase of six million in the fifty years following. It is during the last eighty years, likewise, that the American church has shown its colossal vigor in the inauguration of its missionary enterprises. Beginning with the second decade of our century with a contribution of $200,000, the total amount raised for home and foreign missions in this country up to 1880 was $129,000,000, and 88% of that was raised during the last thirty years; 70,000 mission communicants in 1830 had become 210,000 in 1850, and 850,000 in 1880. All of this, to say nothing of other organizations of evangelization and amelioration, the Bible Society, the Tract Society, and the rest has sprung from the fecund soil of our magnificent Gospel century.

Comments on *1.4.1 Lessons for those who Doubt*:

In reminding my audience of some of the world's thinkers whose names are more or less familiar as of men who were or are distinguished in science, and at the same time believers in Christianity, I named no natives of the neighbouring Republic, though such men abound there, but Canadians are less familiar with them than with the names I have given in the lecture. After the preceding pages were in type it occurred to me to supply the omission by getting needed information from my friend and pastor, the Rev. Dr. Kellogg, a clergyman (I may observe) with a wide and just reputation for varied and accurate learning, and a profound thinker on all subjects with which in his active life he has had to do. The following is from the reply which he was kind enough to send to my application:

> As for distinguished American scientists who have been or are decided believers in Evangelical Christianity, the following names occur to me: Among geologists – First, Professor James B. Dana, of Yale University, to whose authority, if I recollect aright, Mr. Gladstone confidently appealed in one of his recent essays in apologetics; also, Professor G. Frederick Wright, of the University of Oberlin, a scholar whose extensive original research has made him one of the leading authorities on the glacial age on this continent; and, again, Professor Le Conte, of the University of California, another geologist of repute, a decided evolutionist of the *theistic* type, but therewith also a "pronounced" believer. Then might be named Professor Young, of Princeton College, one of the first astronomers in the States; and, in the medical profession, Dr. Willard Park, of New York, not long ago

deceased, commonly reputed to have stood at the head of his profession in surgery; and the late Dr. Agnew, for a long time one of the most distinguished oculists in the States; all of them decided Christian men.

The late Professor Arnold Guyot, of Princeton, who had an enviable reputation as an authority in Physical Geography and Geology on both sides of the Atlantic, it was my privilege for many years to know him as a man of the most devout evangelical spirit. I remember well a remark which I once heard from him in a lecture to my own class in the college, which well shows his position: "Young gentlemen, God has written two books, the book of the Word and the book of the Rocks, and it is perfectly certain that He has written the same thing in both of these books. If, in any case, we are not able to see this distinctly, we must consider that it can only be because our knowledge and understanding of one or both of the two books is as yet imperfect." To these names I might add from a somewhat earlier generation, the late Professor Joseph Henry of the Smithsonian Institute, Washington, DC., and Professor Samuel Morse, whose names are both closely connected with the invention of the electric telegraph; as also many others; but these will probably suffice for your purpose.

I received a subsequent note from Dr. Kellogg, which I have pleasure in adding, as follows:

> I had but just sent my note and enclosure to you this morning, when in one of my papers I found two extracts bearing on the subject of your lecture, which are from

such authority and so excellent, that I take the liberty to send them, thinking that possibly you might like to make use of one or both of them.

The first is from the American poet and man of letters, James Russell Lowell, lately U.S. Minister to Great Britain. If not a scientific man, yet his high reputation as a gentleman of high and broad culture, and of extensive opportunities of observation, will make his words to have weight with many. On a certain public occasion in England several persons had expressed themselves in a contemptuous way regarding Christianity, when Mr. Lowell, in his speech, said: "When the microscopic search of skepticism has turned its attention to human society, and found a spot on this planet ten miles square where a decent man can live in decency, comfort, and security, supporting and educating his children unspoiled and unpolluted, manhood respected, womanhood honoured, and human life held in due regard – when skeptics can find such a place, ten miles square, on this globe, where the Gospel of Christ has not gone and cleared the way, and laid the foundations, and made decency and security possible, it will then be in order for the skeptical literati to move thither, and there ventilate their views."

The second extract is from Professor Mbegard, occupant of the chair of philosophy in the University of Copenhagen, who, until recently, was regarded as one of the chief representatives of philosophic atheism in Denmark. According to the Semeur Vaudois, he has recently published a second edition of his works, in the introduction to which he uses the following words: "The experience of life, its sufferings and griefs, have shaken my soul, and have broken the foundation upon which I formerly thought I could build. Full of faith in the sufficiency of science, I thought to have found in it a sure refuge from all the contingencies of life. This illusion is vanished; when the tempest which plunged me in sorrow, the moorings, the cable of science, broke like thread. Then I seized upon that help which many before me had laid hold of. I sought and found peace in God. Since then I have certainly not abandoned science, but I have assigned to it another place in my life."

Christianity & Its Influence

Sir Oliver Mowat

2.0 Editor's Note

ON SUNDAY FEBRUARY 13, 1898, the Honourable Sir Oliver Mowat was asked to deliver an address to the Young Men's Christian Association (YMCA) of the Medical Faculty of the University of Toronto and of Trinity Medical College on "Christianity & its Influence." The address was later published as a booklet by Mowat, following his *Christianity & its Evidences*.

While the original text of the published manuscript of 1898 has been preserved, small edits have been applied to better facilitate the modern reading experience. For example, chapter headers have been added when there were none, and paragraph breaks were introduced where paragraphs were running longer than a full page. In regard to Scriptural citations, the same wording as the original citation has been maintained.

2.1 The Spirit of the Medical Profession

Students of medicine have chosen for their life-work a profession than which no other, having to do primarily with things earthly, is more honourable, or more useful, or brings to those who follow it a larger amount of esteem, respect and gratitude. How could it be otherwise? The purpose and efforts of the profession are to save life, and to remove or allay pain and misery. That is their business. All of us well know that a medical practitioner, in the exercise of his profession, often knowingly runs great risks, risks to his health, and risks to his life, in visiting and treating patients suffering from contagious and infectious diseases, as well as in other ways; but he no more thinks of preferring his personal safety to the duty which his profession demands of him, than the soldier shrinks from his dangerous duty when called on to face human foes armed for his destruction. By the relief which a medical man gives to his patients, and the attention which they receive from him in the discharge of his duty, he becomes an object of gratitude and affection both to his patients and to others to whom his patients are dear; and in this way he acquires with both classes influence in matters outside his profession.

The fact of his being a man of education above the average of those with whom he has to do is a further occasion of influence with them. His influence from all these causes is both an unsought influence, arising in part from what is known of his character, opinions and opportunities, and also an influence which he may exert by express effort. Whatever the influence is, it is a "talent" to be used for good. Whatever power of this kind you may have, most of you (I hope all of you) would like to employ worthily. That I think I may assume to be the present sentiment of each of you. You would not like to use your influence for harm, nor to throw it away unused for good. You would like that, in some way or other, and in every way practicable, the world may be the better for your having lived in it; that your country may be the better for your having been its citizen; and that your family, your mother and your father, your sisters and your brothers, and all others whom you love or like, may be the better for your relation to them. I should be glad to be able to say something that may help any of you to use in the most beneficial way practicable the influence which you may possess or acquire.

With this object, then, my first remark is, that if in the course of my long and active life I have learned one lesson more distinctly than another, it is that the influence of a man or woman for good, as regards even this world, is immensely promoted by having faith in Christianity. Many of you know that to be so; and many of you are, I hope, acting on that knowledge, and mean to with God's help act on it to the end. It would be delightful if this were the case with all of you. The average medical students and average medical practitioners in our Province are said to compare favourably with the average of such students and practitioners anywhere; and as regards both the learning of the profession and skill in its application. This is gratifying to all Canadians. It would be still more gratifying to all the best of them if it could also be truly said that our medical men, young and old, were distinguished above their fellows throughout the world for hearty acceptance of the Christian faith, and for Christian conduct and character.

There may be some present who, while accepting or professing the Christian faith, do not act upon it; and there may be others who do not give to the religion of the loving Christ even their outward assent. It is to these classes of medical students specially that I purpose speaking, though I shall not have in mind them only.

Some young men, and some who are not young, think it smart to laugh at religion in general, or at some of its doctrines; and this without having studied the subject in (if at all) more than a very partial and superficial manner. I trust that there are no such mockers among you. Such mockery, permit me to say, is rude and foolish conceit on the part of any young people who indulge in it, considering that the subject is of transcendent importance, that the religion of Jesus is and always has been very dear to multitudes of the best people everywhere, and that a great host of men of high intellect and great learning have in all ages believed in it.

People of the present day are encouraged to disbelieve by the authority and example of eminent men (comparatively few in number) who, during the last half-century, have been declared or known unbelievers. The influence, also, of many of the most read novels of the present day is on the same side. These novels are generally read, not for their agnosticism, but for their attractions in other respects, and, while their infidelity may not hurt readers whose faith is established, it is apt to harm others, especially perhaps young men. So it is with many magazines and newspapers conducted with ability, and valuable in other respects, but edited in an anti-Christian spirit, and in which from time to time there appear anti-Christian articles or observations. In some of these publications, as well as in other publications avowedly anti-Christian, it is affirmed, and many of their constant readers are led to believe, that Christianity is a "fable," and that belief in it is "dying out," if it is not "dead." Some go as far as to assert as true the absurdity that Christianity is a hindrance to civilization and to the good of the world, instead of being (as it is) their great promoter. No errors could be greater than these.

While it is true that some eminent men have in this century announced themselves as anti-Christians, some eminent men have done the like in perhaps every age of the Christian era; but there never was a time when a larger number of the educated men of the world were Christians than is the case today. In speaking of eminent men who have been or are believers, need I remind you of such eminent believers as Bacon, and Newton and Brewster, and Faraday, and Agassiz, and Dana, and Morse, amongst physicists who have passed away; or as Lord Kelvin, Mr. Mivart, and Sir William Dawson, amongst physicists who are still living; besides a very host of other learned and able men of the highest distinction in all countries and ages, scientists, philosophers, historians, judges, statesmen, legislators, doctors, lawyers, literary men, and theologians, who have believed in Christianity as a revelation from heaven.

This belief in Christianity by great and good and learned men does not prove Christianity to be true; but, to intelligent inquirers, the belief in it by such men neutralizes and destroys any argument against Christianity derived from the agnosticism of other eminent men, and shows to the intelligent that men must have other reasons for unbelief than the opinions of unbelievers, however eminent.

2.2 The Assumed Death of Christianity

As for Christianity being dead or dying, this is most certainly not true, and can be shown by most satisfactory evidence not to be true. It is the reverse of the truth. A like assertion as to Christianity being in a dying condition was in past ages often made; but the facts always turned out otherwise. The men who some 1860 years ago got the Founder of Christianity put to death, thought that by that act they had extinguished the religion which He taught. But, instead of his religion being extinguished, its adherents increased immensely from that day, both in numbers and in devotion; and so increased far more rapidly than they had done before. So, the early assailants of this religion, after its Founder's death, thought repeatedly that they had destroyed it, if not by arguments, yet by martyrdoms and by persecutions of the fiercest kinds. But all failed.

Voltaire, in the eighteenth century, believed and prophesied that "before the beginning of the nineteenth century Christianity will have disappeared from the earth." The beginning of the nineteenth century came, and Christianity had not disappeared. We are now near the end of that century, and Christianity not only still exists, but never before showed greater evidences of both life and permanency. Never before had so large a number of the world's population faith in some form of Christianity as is the case now. A century ago the Christian population of the world (using here the word "Christian" in its broadest sense) was estimated at less than 200 million; it is now upwards of 400 million. There never was a time, either, (as I said on another occasion) in which, among Christians, there were so many true, earnest and self-denying believers as now; never a time when the churches, old and new, were more active and aggressive; never a time when so many Christian organizations of great power were at work for the evangelization of the world; never a time in which so much money was contributed to Christian objects of all kinds.

While in all these respects there has been a great increase in the religious activity, and religious attainments generally, of the old churches, the number of new and powerful organizations which have sprung up with like objects is most remarkable. Some of these are independent of particular churches, and others are in close connection with existing churches. It is only about 150 years since the Methodists came into existence as a separate organization, and they have now become one of the greatest Protestant denominations in Christendom. Sunday-schools for religious training are of still more modern origin; and it is estimated that the number of scholars now receiving instruction in them is nearly twenty-three million; a most significant fact, seeing that

Sunday-schools are amongst the most powerful agencies of the Christian faith.

The British and Foreign Bible Society has been said to be the greatest agency ever devised for the diffusion of the Holy Scriptures, and it had no existence until the present century. The Young Men's Christian Associations are of still more recent origin than these societies, and are now in active operation in almost every part of the world. The same may be said of the Women's Christian Associations of various kinds, the Societies of Christian Endeavor, the Epworth Leagues, the Salvation Army, and other new Christian enterprises. These are Protestant institutions. I think I see, also, amongst Roman Catholics, increased interest during the same period in those great truths which, happily, Roman Catholics and Protestants hold in common. The progress of Christianity includes both Roman Catholics and Protestants.

2.3 The Influence of Christianity

So, modern missions have been in operation for but a century, and now the great missionary societies at work are reckoned by the hundred, and their operations extend to all parts of heathendom, and have been attended with much success amongst heathen peoples. Protestant missions have at work an estimated force of nearly ten thousand foreign missionaries, and more than fifty thousand native missionaries. This great army of Christian workers minister to 1,250,000 communicants in mission churches, and have three or four million (some estimate five million) of adherents who were previously heathen.

Through the agency of missions, some lands which a century ago and less were heathen lands are now distinctly Christian. These missions have also accomplished much incidentally that is valuable to the human race with reference to this life, as well as accomplishing much in regard to the infinitely more important matter of the life to come. They have accomplished great things in all the departments of knowledge, learning and science; great things in advancing civilization and all that civilization implies; and great things in promoting morality, a matter more important than all others relating to this life. On this subject I find the following cited from the testimony of Lord Lawrence, who was Viceroy and Governor-General of India from 1864 to 1869, and had thirty years' previous experience there: "I believe, notwithstanding all that the English people have done more than all other agencies combined." Also the following from Sir Bartle Frere, formerly Governor of Bombay, and afterwards of the Cape of Good Hope:

> I assure you that, whatever you have been told to the contrary, the teachings of Christianity amongst the one hundred and sixty million of civilized, industrious Hindus and Mohammedans in India, have effected changes, moral, social and political, which for extent and rapidity of effect are far more extraordinary than anything else you or your fathers have witnessed in modern Europe.

The same thing may be said, and in at least some cases with equal force, as to all other countries in which Christian missionaries have been at work. In a word, the facts place it beyond well-founded doubt that "Christian missionaries are the most effective means ever brought to bear upon the social, civil, commercial, moral and spiritual interests of mankind." The truth of Christianity and faith in it have produced these results.

Some suppose that Christianity has fallen back in the United States, and thence infer that it has fallen back everywhere. But it has not fallen back in the United States, any more than elsewhere. In saying this I put out of account the unchristian hate towards the Motherland manifested by many among our neighbours; and I put out of account the efforts which have been made to keep up or intensify that hate. I know of no sufficient reason for believing that the hate is shared by the religious people of the nation; and it is impossible to believe that the better part of the population, whether religious or not, desire to shed the blood and wreck the property of their kinsmen of another nationality, with whom for seventy years and more there have been peace and friendly relations. As to faith in Christianity in that country, official census returns and other well-authenticated data show that, notwithstanding all the irreligion which prevails there as it does elsewhere, Christianity is more full of life in the United States now than it ever was before; that its vitality has increased in every decade of the century; and has so increased not only absolutely, but also relatively to the population.

This appears from, for example, what has been ascertained of the comparative number of churches at different periods, the comparative accommodation afforded, the comparative number of church members, evangelical ministers, Sunday-school teachers and Sunday-school pupils, the comparative value of church property, and the comparative amounts contributed annually for missions and other religious objects.

Thus, so far from there having been a dying out of Christianity in the United States or elsewhere, ascertained facts show greatly increased life and vigour there and throughout the world, and make plain that, rampant as agnosticism or unbelief may seem in some respects to be, if any of you have been inclined on that account, or any other, to regard Christianity as a dying belief or a dying institution, you are deceiving yourselves. The truth is the very reverse.

2.4 The Influence of Christianity (Continued)

Undoubtedly, though Christianity has been steadily advancing, yet there is at the same time, unhappily, much irreligion in all nominally Christian lands; but this is not a new thing; there has always been irreligion; and so, as Christians generally believe, there will continue to be until Christ comes in person to reign on the earth. This irreligion is, in part, in the form of intellectual unbelief; but it is much more in the form of crime, vice, injustice, cruelty, falsehood and selfishness of every kind – all of which Christianity condemns, and has declared war against. A religion which is so exacting in its demands as Christianity is, and was so unpromising at its beginning, and yet has spread as Christianity has done, and has so strong a hold on mankind at this day, is certainly not dead, is not dying, is not a failure.

It is undoubtedly an exacting religion, as well as a true and the only true religion; but its exactions are such as promote the present as well as future well-being of the race; for, what is it that Christianity requires of us? It requires personal purity and godliness. As regards conduct towards others, it requires that in every act of life each of us enquire: What does honesty require? What do justice and fair-dealing require of us? What does humanity require of us? What does the influence of our example require of us? As regards example, you young men may by your example help to make or keep your companions and others sober men, well-behaved in all the relations of life, and for all their lives; or, on the other hand, you may help to make them drunkards, and in other respects worse than useless to themselves and to their families and to society. My brothers, which will you do? Will you help them to be good and useful? Or will you help them to be bad, and worse than useless? Will you be on Christ's side? Or will you be on His enemy's?

What is revealed or believed of rewards and punishments in another world has a powerful effect on multitudes who do not appreciate other Christian truths, and exerts some influence on those also who do appreciate those other truths. As to the rewards, Professor Huxley, agnostic as he is (unhappily), writing on the subject of "Decline in Religious Belief," has this just observation:

> The lover of moral beauty, struggling through a world of sorrow and sin, is surely as much the stronger for believing that sooner or later a vision of perfect peace and goodness will burst upon him, as a toiler up a mountain is the stronger for the belief that beyond the crag and snow lie rest and home.

So, belief in future punishment frightens many, and restrains them from wrong-doing more than anything else does. Everlasting punishment certainly is a fate which no present advantages or pleasures can compensate for, even though these should last a lifetime; and no earthly advantage or pleasure lasts a lifetime. So, immortality in happiness is infinitely more than an adequate reward for any amount of work and sacrifice and suffering in our earthly lives, however long these may last. No consideration outside of religion can present such powerful reasons for right living as are afforded by the credited declarations of Scripture regarding rewards and punishments.

But Christianity presents far more powerful motives than rewards and punishments. It does so in teaching that God is love, and is to those who love Him the most loveable of all objects of love. According to Christian doctrine, God is nearer to us than father or mother, than wife or child, than brother or sister; we owe to Him all things; He is our Creator, our Redeemer, our Preserver, our Bountiful Benefactor; He so loved the world – so loved us – as to send into the world His only begotten and eternal Son to be a propitiation for our sins. It was from love to us that Christ came into the world, and suffered, and died; and, as a result, whoever now believes in Him, and earnestly and truly accepts Him, shall have an everlasting life of unspeakable joy and happiness and purity. This loving God is to be loved with all the heart and soul and mind and strength; this, our Saviour declared, is the first and greatest commandment; and the second, He said, is like unto it – thou shalt love thy neighbour as thyself. On these two commandments, He declared, hang all the law and the prophets; and this (we are told) is the love of God, namely, that we keep His commandments.

This commandment have we from Him, that he who loveth God do love his neighbour also; we are to love our neighbour as Christ loved all men, and gave himself a sacrifice for them. In discharging this duty we are to bear one another's burdens, and therein fulfill the law of Christ. We are to render glad and loving service in a special sense to the friendless, the sick, the suffering, and the needy, whatever their country or their creed. The Samaritan is to help and do good to the Jew, and the Jew is to help and do good to the Samaritan; Britons to Americans; Americans to Britons. In a word, Christianity enjoins on all to cultivate supreme love to the God and Father of all, and to live towards all men lives of truth, justice, kindness, and active benevolence. That is what God loves, and requires of us.

Without this love on our part, and this goodness of character and conduct towards our fellow men, it is the doctrine of Christianity that the soundness of our faith is nothing – is but as sounding brass and a tinkling cymbal; and is so even though that faith were strong enough as (in the language of the great apostle of the Gentiles) to "remove mountains."

It is thus to love, that supreme importance is attached by Christianity. The Christian religion is a religion of love; and of all that love involves. Love is the sweetest of all words in human language. Love is the most powerful motive power with mankind of every class. All history and all experience show this. Love makes practicable, and even easy and pleasant, what would otherwise be difficult, or impossible, or intolerably disagreeable. So it has been amongst all peoples and in all ages.

How can it be otherwise than promotive of good to really and from the heart believe that our Creator, the Creator of all things, the all-seeing God of the universe, is a God of Love? And is on the side of everything good? Desires us to be loving to one another, and to be good, honest, truthful, pure? Knows and notices when we are so, and when we are not so? Loves in a special way those who are good and kind and true? And will endow these with great blessings in the eternal life to come? How can belief in such truths as these be otherwise than good in its influence on a man who believes? How can it be otherwise than good for mankind as a whole?

The influence of Christianity on the character of men is under God owing, not to its moral teachings merely, but, in connection with these moral teachings, is owing to the facts and doctrines of Christianity. These give incalculable force to the moral teachings. As the result of Christian teachings, the actual historical fact is, that loving faith in our Heavenly Father and His eternal Son has, in the case of millions of Christian men and women in the last nineteen centuries, been a great and mighty power for good; and it is a great and mighty power for good; and it is a great and mighty power for good still; and so, doubtless, will be forever.

The faith of all believers in Christianity is not equally strong, nor is the obedience of all equally full. It is a doctrine of the Church to which I belong that, "no mere man since the fall is able in this life perfectly to keep the commandments of God, but doth daily break them in thought, word and deed." I believe that no important Christian denomination teaches the absolute and uninterrupted sinlessness of Christians, not of even the best of them. On the contrary, all Christian churches concur in holding that any Christian may be "overtaken in a fault," as St. Peter was when he denied his Master, and on other occasions. The like was the case with some Old Testament saints and worthies. But when a Christian has sinned he remembers his sin with shame and humiliation; and his comfort is, that before God, sin that is repented of is sin that is forgiven; that if we confess our sins, we are assured our Heavenly Father is "faithful and just to forgive our sins and to cleanse us from all unrighteousness"; that "if any man sin we have an advocate with the Father, Jesus Christ, the Righteous"; and that he is the propitiation for our sins; and not for ours only, but also for the sins of the whole world.[1] In dealing with such cases, St. Paul gave this direction: "Brethren, if a man be overtaken in a fault, ye who are spiritual restore such a one in the spirit of meekness; considering thyself, lest thou also be tempted."

While absolute perfection of conduct or character may not be attained or attainable by any person in this life, experience has shown that none can really believe the doctrines which Christ taught, and in any degree really love Him, the God-man, the Divine Messenger of Love, without being in some measure influenced by their faith in Him, and manifesting in their lives and character something of the Christian spirit. Love to God and to Christ the Son, begets likeness to the character which God approves and Christ exemplified; and, though a Christian may not be perfect, his efforts are in the direction of perfection. It is a matter of certain fact that millions have loved, and millions are loving, the Father and Son sufficiently to strive with all their hearts to conform themselves (by God's grace) to all Christ's teachings; and that multitudes in all ages have demonstrated the power of Christianity over the heart and conduct by enduring for its sake the greatest possible hardships, sacrifices and sufferings. It is interesting to

---

[1] When Mowat refers to "ours", as opposed to the universal body of believers, he is referring instead to his immediate audience. As to the use of the word "world", Mowat was not a universalist, having been educated in the Christian reformed tradition, he understood this term as referring to God's elect of every nation and tongue.

note that every form of Christianity has had its martyrs for the sake of the Lord Jesus Christ.

2.5 Concluding Remarks

As to Christianity being a hindrance to the well-being of the race, as some allow themselves to think or say, the proposition sounds supremely absurd to most men of fair minds, whether they are Christians or not. Thomas Carlyle did not believe in Christianity as a revealed and supernatural religion; but he said of it: "The Christian religion must ever be regarded as the crowning glory, or, rather, the life and soul, of our whole modern culture." So Mathew Arnold, though very far from being an orthodox Christian, had such words as these to say of the Christian religion and its influence:

> Men are not mistaken in thinking that Christianity has done them good, [are not mistaken] in loving it, in wishing to listen to those who will talk to them about what they love, and (they) will talk of it with admiration and gratitude… Christianity is truly… the greatest and happiest stroke ever yet made for human perfection. Men do not err, they are on firm ground of experience, when they say that they have practically found Christianity to be something incomparably beneficent.

Then again, Mr. Lecky, the rationalist historian, recently elected to the British House of Commons as member for the University of Dublin, has these observations:

> Christianity, the life of morality, the basis of civilization, has regenerated the world… It (the Christian religion)

softens the character, purifies and directs the imagination, blends insensibly with habitual modes of thought, and, without revolutionizing, gives a tone and bias to all forms of action... As a matter of fact, Christianity has done more to quicken the affections of mankind, to create a pure and merciful idea, than any other influence that has ever acted upon the world... The great characteristic of Christianity is that it has been the main source of the moral development of Europe, and that it has discharged this office, not so much by the inculcation of a system of ethics, however pure, as by the assimilating and attractive influence of a perfect ideal. The moral progress of mankind can never cease to be distinctively and intensely Christian as long as it consists of a gradual approximation to the character of the Christian Founder. There is, indeed, nothing more wonderful in the history of the human race than the way in which that ideal has traversed the lapse of ages, acquiring new strength and beauty with each advance of civilization, and infusing its beneficent influence into every sphere of thought and action.

No; the Christianity of the Bible is no hindrance to humanity or human progress; it is the intensely opposite of a hindrance; it is a mighty power, the mightiest of all powers, for purifying and humanizing and civilizing, as well as for preparing for the blessedness of an immortal life in heaven.

In view of these considerations, if Christianity were not true, a lover of his race might well regret with all his heart that it is not true; but a candid, intelligent examination of its evidences satisfies most enquirers that

Christianity is true. If any of you think at present that these evidences do not demonstrate its truth, let it be remembered that many learned men and good men have thought, and still think, the demonstration ample. But what if the evidences amount to a greater or lesser degree of probability only? Do not throw away your faith on that account. There is no young man or woman, no man or woman young or old, who does not believe, and rightly believe, a hundred things on grounds of probability, which, to say the least, are inferior to those probabilities that favour Christianity. Why is any young man unwilling to believe in Christianity on like probable evidence? Why does he allow himself to treat as nothing the testimony which there is in its favour, whether in his opinion such evidence amount to demonstration or not? Why should he stumble at some supposed difficulty, in the evidence or otherwise, for which he cannot find what may seem to him a satisfactory solution?

There are difficulties in everything. There are difficulties and mysteries in every branch of science; in every department of nature; in the functions of our bodies; in the workings of our minds. Even in mathematics, the science of demonstration, there are things which are true and yet incomprehensible. What though if there are difficulties and mysteries in Christianity also? If it presents difficulties and mysteries, consider also what the evidences are in its favour. Let these be studied and weighed. Its proofs are many and various. Among Christians who have examined them, some are more impressed with one line of evidence and some with another. In an address which I delivered elsewhere some time ago, and which was afterwards published, I gave a summary of the proofs which were then most satisfactory to my own mind. Others may prefer some of the other proofs which published treatises supply. It is only necessary that every man should be fully persuaded in his own mind.

As the conclusion of the whole matter, my sisters and brothers, I exhort you, being as a layman one of yourselves, that you hold fast the Christian faith as being a faith necessary and good for both worlds; for this world, as we know; and for the next world, as for strong reasons, and in common with a multitude of the world's greatest thinkers and best men and women, we heartily believe. Hold fast to the Christian faith, as good for yourselves, good for those whom you love, and good for those whom from time to time you may influence. Above all, hold fast to your Christian faith from gratitude and love to the loving Father and God of all, and to His loving Son, who from love laid down his life for us.

My sisters and brothers, think on these things; and may the Spirit of the Eternal Father have His abode in your minds and hearts forever.

About the Contributor

Steven R. Martins is the founding director of the Cántaro Institute and founding pastor of Sevilla Chapel in St. Catharines, Ontario, Canada. A second-generation Canadian, Steven is of Ibero-American parentage and has worked in the fields of missional apologetics and church leadership for eight years. He has spoken at numerous conferences, churches, and University student events, from York University, Toronto, to the University of West Indies in Port of Spain, Trinidad, and the national Universities of Costa Rica (UNCR and UNC), and the Evangelical University of El Salvador. He has also contributed articles to Coalición por el Evangelio (TGC in Spanish) and the *Siglo XXI* journal of Editorial CLIR.

Steven holds a Master's degree *summa cum laude* in Theological Studies with a focus on Christian apologetics from Veritas International University (Santa Ana, CA., USA) and a Bachelor of Human Resource Management from York University (Toronto, ON., Canada). Steven has served on the executive board for Answers in Genesis Canada, and has served with the Ezra Institute for Contemporary Christianity (EICC) as a staff apologist, writer and director of ministry development and advancement (DMDA) for four years. He has also served pastorally at Harbour Fellowship Church in St. Catharines. Steven is married to Cindy and lives in Jordan Station, Ontario, with their children Matthias and Timothy.

www.ingramcontent.com/pod-product-compliance
Lightning Source LLC
LaVergne TN
LVHW040152080526
838202LV00042B/3126